CRYPTO TAXATION

CA KUSHAL SONI

ISBN
Paperback 979-8-89906-324-4
Hardcase 979-8-89929-269-9

CONTENTS

Contents

INTRODUCTION

The global trend towards deregulation and increased flexibility has paved the way for the emergence of a wide array of cryptocurrencies and virtual assets. These digital assets, operating outside the confines of traditional financial systems, offer new opportunities for investment, trade, and financial interaction. However, their decentralized nature and the rapid pace of their development also pose significant challenges for regulators and financial institutions alike. As the world grapples with the implications of this new digital frontier, the need for clear and adaptable regulatory frameworks becomes ever more pressing.

Governments around the world maintain strict control over their respective currencies. This control serves a multitude of purposes, including but not limited to, regulation of domestic and international markets, curbing terrorism and other unlawful activities, and preventing money laundering. India is no exception to this global practice. The Reserve Bank of India, the country's central banking institution, has not yet officially recognized cryptocurrency as legal tender.

This lack of official recognition stems from a variety of concerns that the government and regulatory bodies have regarding cryptocurrencies. These concerns include the decentralized nature of cryptocurrencies, which makes them difficult to regulate, their potential for use in illicit activities, and the volatility of their value.

CRYPTOCURRENCY HISTORY

The advent of Bitcoin in 2009, marked by the mining of the Genesis Block by Satoshi Nakamoto, heralded a new era in the world of finance and technology. This groundbreaking event not only introduced the world to Bitcoin, the first and most well-known cryptocurrency, but also laid the foundation for the development of a whole new asset class: virtual digital assets.

The creation of the Genesis Block was the culmination of years of research and development in the field of cryptography and computer science. It was the first practical implementation of a decentralized, peer-to-peer electronic cash system, which had been theorized for years but never successfully realized.

The significance of the Genesis Block lies not only in its technical innovation but also in its philosophical and economic implications. It challenged the traditional centralized model of money and finance, offering a new vision of a decentralized, trustless system where individuals could transact directly with each other without the need for intermediaries.

The birth of Bitcoin and the subsequent emergence of other cryptocurrencies have sparked a global debate about the future of money, finance, and the role of technology in shaping our economic systems. While the long-term impact of these developments remains to be seen, there is no doubt that the creation of the Genesis Block was a seminal moment in the history of finance and technology, with far-reaching implications for the future.

Evolution of cryptocurrency and Bitcoin:

2008	2009	2010	2011	2021	2024
Sato hi Nakamoto issued Bitcoin white paper	Creation of Bitcoin First blockchain launched	First transaction in Bitcoin	Bitcoin price cross $1	$3 Trillion value of all crypto-currency in existence	$3.45 Trillion value of all crypto-currency in existence

CENTRAL BANK DIGITAL CURRENCY (CBDC)

The emergence of Central Bank Digital Currencies (CBDCs) signifies a notable advancement in the evolution of virtual currencies. As announced in the Union Budget 2022 by the Government of India, the introduction of CBDCs in India is poised to reshape the financial landscape by potentially replacing physical cash within the next decade. This strategic move towards a cashless economy holds significant implications for the future of transactions and financial interactions in the country.

CBDCs, being digital representations of a country's fiat currency issued and backed by the central bank, offer several potential advantages over traditional cash and existing digital payment methods. They can enable faster, cheaper, and more secure transactions, while also enhancing financial inclusion and accessibility. Additionally, CBDCs can provide central banks with greater control over monetary policy and potentially mitigate risks associated with private cryptocurrencies.

However, the implementation of CBDCs also raises important considerations around privacy, security, and potential impacts on the banking sector and financial stability. As governments and central banks around the world explore the development and adoption of CBDCs, careful planning and consideration of these factors will be crucial to ensure a smooth and successful transition towards a digital currency future.

FINANCIAL ACTION TASK FORCE ON VIRTUAL ASSETS

The Financial Action Task Force (FATF), an international body established to combat money laundering and the financing of terrorism, has formulated a definition for 'virtual assets' within the context of cryptocurrencies. According to the FATF, a virtual asset is a digital representation of value that can be digitally traded or transferred, and can also be utilized for payment or investment purposes.

This definition encompasses a wide array of digital assets that are used as a medium of exchange or store of value, including but not limited to cryptocurrencies like Bitcoin, Ethereum, and Litecoin, as well as other digital tokens and assets that can be traded or transferred electronically.

Virtual assets, also known as digital assets or cryptocurrencies, are digital representations of value that can be stored, transferred, or traded electronically. These assets exist exclusively in electronic form and are typically secured by cryptographic techniques, ensuring their integrity and authenticity.

KEY CHARACTERISTICS AND TYPES OF VIRTUAL ASSETS

- **Cryptocurrencies:** These are digital or virtual currencies that utilize cryptography for security and operate independently of a central bank or government. Examples include Bitcoin, Ethereum, and Litecoin.

- **Utility Tokens:** These tokens represent access to a specific product or service within a blockchain-based platform. They are often used to raise funds during Initial Coin Offerings (ICOs).

- **Security Tokens:** These tokens represent ownership in a company or asset and may offer rights such as dividends or voting rights. They are subject to securities regulations in many jurisdictions.

- **Non-Fungible Tokens (NFTs):** These tokens represent unique digital assets, such as artwork, collectibles, or virtual real estate. Each NFT has distinct properties and cannot be exchanged for another NFT on a one-to-one basis.

DECENTRALIZATION AND BLOCKCHAIN TECHNOLOGY

Virtual assets often operate on decentralized networks, such as blockchain, which are distributed ledgers that record transactions across multiple computers. This decentralization eliminates the need for a central authority and offers increased transparency and security.

Use Cases and Applications:

Virtual assets have a wide range of use cases and applications, including:

- **Payments and Remittances:** Cryptocurrencies can be used for peer-to-peer payments and cross-border remittances, often with lower fees and faster transaction times compared to traditional financial systems.

- **Investment and Trading:** Virtual assets are traded on various exchanges and can be held as investment assets. Their value can fluctuate significantly, offering potential for high returns but also carrying significant risks.

- **Decentralized Finance (DeFi):** Virtual assets are used in DeFi applications, which offer financial services such as lending, borrowing, and trading without intermediaries.

- **Gaming and Virtual Worlds:** Virtual assets are used in gaming and virtual worlds to represent in-game items, currencies, or virtual real estate.

- **Supply Chain Management:** Blockchain-based systems can track the movement of goods and assets throughout the supply chain, increasing transparency and reducing fraud.

REGULATORY LANDSCAPE AND CHALLENGES

The regulatory landscape for virtual assets is evolving rapidly, with different jurisdictions adopting varying approaches. Some countries have embraced virtual assets and developed clear regulatory frameworks, while others have imposed restrictions or outright bans. Key regulatory challenges include:

- **Consumer Protection:** Ensuring that investors and users of virtual assets are protected from fraud, scams, and market manipulation.

- **Anti-Money Laundering (AML) and Combating the Financing of Terrorism (CFT):** Preventing the use of virtual assets for illicit activities.

- **Taxation:** Developing clear tax policies for virtual assets, including income tax, capital gains tax, and goods and services tax (GST).

- **Financial Stability:** Assessing and mitigating potential risks to financial stability posed by virtual assets.

Future Potential and Impact:

Virtual assets have the potential to disrupt traditional financial systems and revolutionize various industries. However, their future impact will depend on factors such as regulatory developments, technological advancements, and market adoption.

Important Concepts:

Blockchain:

A blockchain is a distributed ledger system that stores and transmits data in blocks that are linked together sequentially, forming a digital chain. Each block contains a timestamp and a link to the previous block, creating an immutable and transparent record of all transactions.

How Blockchain Works – Diagramatic Presentation

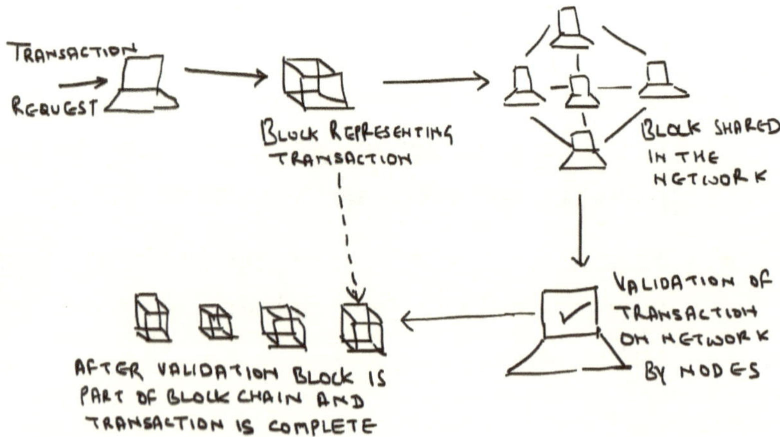

Key Characteristics of Blockchain:

- **Decentralization:** Unlike traditional databases that are controlled by a central authority, blockchains are distributed across a network of nodes. This eliminates the need for a trusted third party and makes the system resistant to censorship and manipulation.

- **Immutability:** Once data is recorded on a blockchain, it cannot be altered or deleted. This ensures the integrity of the data and prevents fraud.

- **Transparency:** All transactions on a blockchain are visible to all participants. This creates a high level of transparency and accountability.

- **Security:** Blockchains use cryptographic algorithms to secure data and prevent unauthorized access.

How Blockchain Works:

- **Transactions:** Users initiate transactions on the blockchain network.

- **Verification:** Nodes on the network verify the transactions using cryptographic algorithms.

- **Block Creation:** Verified transactions are grouped into a block.

- **Consensus:** Nodes reach a consensus on the validity of the block.

- **Block Addition:** The block is added to the blockchain.

Applications of Blockchain:

Blockchain technology has a wide range of potential applications beyond cryptocurrencies. Some of the most promising use cases include:

- **Supply Chain Management:** Blockchain can be used to track the movement of goods and ensure the authenticity of products.

- **Healthcare:** Blockchain can be used to securely store and share medical records.

- **Voting:** Blockchain can be used to create a secure and transparent voting system.

- **Identity Management:** Blockchain can be used to create a self-sovereign identity system.

Overall, blockchain technology has the potential to revolutionize a wide range of industries by providing a secure, transparent, and efficient way to store and manage data.

Distributed Ledger Technology (DLT):

The World Bank Group provides a comprehensive definition of Distributed Ledger Technology (DLT), recognizing its innovative and rapidly evolving nature. DLT is described as a groundbreaking approach to data recording and sharing. It involves multiple data stores, referred to as ledgers, which are distributed across a network.

A key characteristic of DLT is that each ledger within the network maintains an identical copy of the data records. This ensures data consistency and integrity across the entire system. The maintenance and control of these ledgers are achieved through a distributed network of computer servers, known as nodes. These nodes work collaboratively to validate and update the data, eliminating the need for a central authority.

DLT's decentralized nature and data replication across multiple nodes offer enhanced security, transparency, and immutability. This technology has the potential to revolutionize various industries by enabling secure and efficient data sharing, reducing costs, and increasing trust among participants.

Distributed Ledger – Diagram

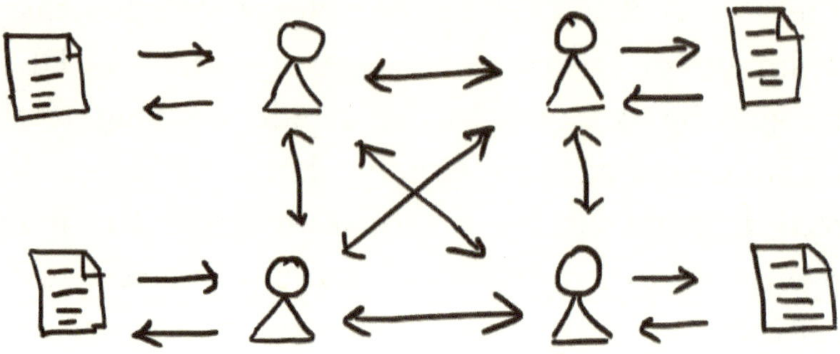

Centralised Ledger – Diagram

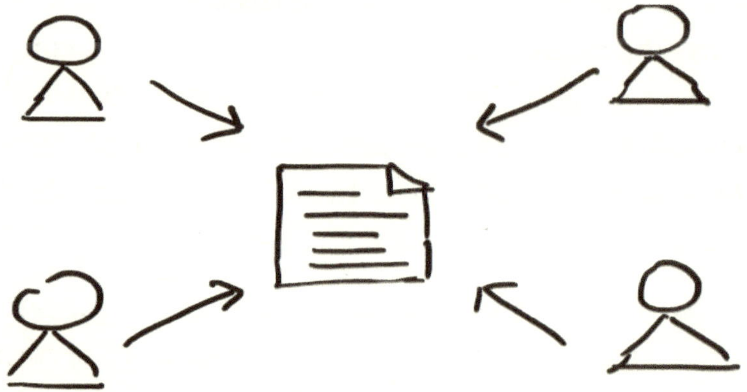

Non-Fungible Tokens (NFTs):

In the realm of digital assets, Non-Fungible Tokens (NFTs) stand out due to their unique characteristic of being non-fungible. The term "non-fungible" signifies that each NFT is distinct and cannot be replaced with another. Unlike fungible assets like cryptocurrencies, where one Bitcoin is interchangeable with another

Bitcoin, NFTs are irreplaceable due to their unique digital identities.

NFTs can encompass a wide array of digital files, including photos, videos, images, animations, and audio files. Each NFT represents ownership or proof of authenticity of the underlying digital asset. This uniqueness and verifiability have made NFTs popular in various fields, such as digital art, collectibles, gaming, and virtual real estate.

The non-fungible nature of NFTs enables creators to tokenize their digital creations and sell them directly to collectors or enthusiasts. This disintermediation of traditional marketplaces allows creators to retain greater control over their work and potentially earn higher royalties from secondary sales.

While NFTs offer exciting possibilities for creators and collectors, it's important to note that the value of an NFT is largely determined by market demand and perception. The scarcity and uniqueness of an NFT can contribute to its value, but ultimately, it's the market that decides the price.

MEANING OF VIRTUAL DIGITAL ASSET (VDA) AS PER SECTION 2(47A) OF THE INCOME-TAX ACT, 1961

'"Virtual digital asset" means–

- any information or code or number or token (not being Indian currency or foreign currency), generated through cryptographic means or otherwise, by whatever name called, providing a digital representation of value exchanged with or without consideration, with the promise or representation of having inherent value, or functions as a store of value or a unit of account including its use in any financial transaction or investment, but not limited to investment scheme; and can be transferred, stored or traded electronically;

- a non-fungible token or any other token of similar nature, by whatever name called;

- any other digital asset, as the Central Government may, by notification in the Official Gazette specify:

Provided that the Central Government may, by notification in the Official Gazette, exclude any digital asset from the definition of virtual digital asset subject to such conditions as may be specified therein.

Explanation—For the purposes of this clause,

- "non-fungible token" means such digital asset as the Central Government may, by notification in the Official Gazette, specify;

- the expressions "currency", "foreign currency" and "Indian currency" shall have the same meanings as respectively assigned to them in clauses (h), (m) and (q) of section 2 of the Foreign Exchange Management Act, 1999.'

IS BONUS, EXCHANGE COINS, POINTS, ETC ARE TREATED AS VDAs?

Businesses and online platforms often incentivize customer loyalty and repeat purchases by offering rewards in the form of bonus coins, exchange coins, points, super coins, or virtual cash. These rewards can typically be redeemed for discounts on future purchases or, in some cases, converted into fiat currency.

These digital rewards are generated through cryptographic processes, ensuring security and uniqueness. They possess inherent value and can sometimes be transferred or traded electronically, similar to other forms of virtual digital assets (VDAs).

In the context of taxation and regulation, these coins or points are considered VDAs if they meet the criteria specified in Section 2(47A). This classification is crucial in determining how these rewards are treated for tax purposes, including potential capital gains or income tax implications.

Therefore, it is essential for businesses and customers to understand the nature of these digital rewards and their potential tax implications. Proper accounting and reporting are necessary to ensure compliance with tax regulations and avoid potential penalties.

NFTs ARE VDAs?

Non-Fungible Tokens (NFTs):

NFTs, or any other token of a similar nature, regardless of the name given to them, are classified as virtual digital assets. This encompasses a broad range of digital items that represent ownership or proof of authenticity of a unique asset. They are distinct from fungible tokens like cryptocurrencies, as they cannot be exchanged on a like-for-like basis due to their unique characteristics.

Key Points:

- **Unique and Non-Interchangeable:** Each NFT has distinct properties, making them non-fungible and not directly replaceable by another token.

- **Ownership and Authenticity:** NFTs often represent ownership of digital art, collectibles, virtual real estate, and other unique digital assets, providing proof of authenticity and provenance.

- **Blockchain-Based:** NFTs are typically built on blockchain technology, which ensures transparency, security, and immutability of ownership records.

- **Diverse Applications:** Beyond digital art and collectibles, NFTs have potential applications in gaming, supply chain management, intellectual property, and various other industries.

- **Tax Implications:** As virtual digital assets, NFTs are subject to taxation in many jurisdictions. The tax treatment may vary depending on factors such as the nature of the NFT, the holding period, and the applicable tax laws.

Remember: The classification of NFTs as virtual digital assets has significant implications for their legal and tax treatment. It is essential to stay informed about the evolving regulatory landscape.

Non-fungible tokens (NFTs) are unique digital assets that represent ownership or proof of authenticity of a particular item or piece of content. These tokens are not interchangeable with one another, unlike cryptocurrencies like Bitcoin, which are fungible.

While the concept of NFTs exists and is recognized within the context of taxation and digital assets, the specific definition and regulatory framework surrounding them is still evolving. **Currently, the Central Government of India has not yet officially notified or specified any particular digital asset as an NFT.** This means that there is no definitive list or set of criteria to determine which digital assets qualify as NFTs for taxation or regulatory purposes.

This lack of specific notification and classification creates a degree of ambiguity and uncertainty for individuals and businesses dealing with NFTs in India. It is important to stay informed about potential updates and clarifications from the Central Government regarding the classification and taxation of NFTs.

NFTs, or Non-Fungible Tokens, can be created for a wide range of digital files, including images, videos, audio files, and other digital assets. These unique tokens are often associated with art, sports, animations, entertainment, and gaming, representing ownership of a specific digital item.

However, it's important to note that only those NFTs specifically notified by the Central Government will be classified as Virtual Digital Assets (VDAs) in India. This distinction is not the same for crypto assets, as all crypto assets, regardless of notification, are considered VDAs. This means that while all crypto assets fall under the purview of VDA regulations, only specific NFTs designated by the government will be treated as such.

Residuary Clause for Other Digital Assets:

In addition to the explicitly defined virtual digital assets, the law includes a residuary clause that empowers the

Central Government to notify and include any other digital asset under the umbrella of "virtual digital asset." This clause acts as a safety net, ensuring that the regulatory framework remains adaptable and can encompass new and emerging forms of digital assets that may not fit the existing definitions.

This flexibility is crucial in the rapidly evolving landscape of digital assets, where innovation constantly introduces new types of assets and tokens. By granting the Central Government the authority to expand the scope of virtual digital assets, the law ensures that the tax regime remains relevant and effective in capturing the value generated by these new and emerging assets.

EXCLUSIONS FROM VDAs

Indian Currency:

Indian Currency and Virtual Digital Assets (VDAs):

In the context of India's cryptocurrency regulations, it's crucial to distinguish between Indian currency and Virtual Digital Assets (VDAs). **Indian currency** is explicitly excluded from the definition of a VDA. This distinction has significant implications for taxation and regulatory compliance.

What constitutes Indian Currency?

As per Section 2(q) of the Foreign Exchange Management Act, 1999 (FEMA Act), Indian currency is defined as any currency expressed or drawn in Indian Rupees. However, there are specific exclusions:

- **Special Bank Notes and Special One Rupee Notes:** These notes, issued under Section 28A of the Reserve Bank of India Act, 1934 (RBI Act), are not considered Indian currency for the purposes of VDA classification.

Key Implications:

- **Taxation:** VDAs are subject to specific tax regulations, including the 30% tax on income from the transfer of VDAs and the 1% TDS on such transactions. Since Indian currency is not classified as a VDA, it is not subject to these tax provisions.

- **Regulatory Compliance:** VDAs are also subject to various regulatory requirements, including KYC/AML norms and reporting obligations. These regulations do not apply to Indian currency transactions.

Important Note: While Indian currency itself is not a VDA, it can be used to purchase VDAs. The conversion of Indian currency to VDA would trigger the tax and regulatory implications associated with VDAs.

According to Section 2(h) of the Foreign Exchange Management Act (FEMA) 1999, the term "Currency" has a broad definition. It encompasses all currency notes, which are the physical paper money we use daily. Additionally, it includes postal notes and postal orders, which are methods of sending money through the postal service.

The definition also covers money orders, which are similar to postal orders but can be issued by various financial institutions. Cheques, drafts, and traveler's cheques are also included, representing different forms of negotiable instruments used for payment.

Furthermore, letters of credit and bills of exchange, which are commonly used in international trade, fall under the purview of "Currency." Promissory notes, which are written promises to pay a specified amount of money, are also encompassed.

The definition extends to credit cards and other similar instruments that may be notified by the Reserve Bank of India (RBI). This gives the RBI the authority to expand the definition and include new forms of payment that may emerge in the future.

'Currency Notes', as per section 2(i) of the FEMA 1999, means and includes cash in the form of coins and bank notes. The Finance Act, 2022 has inserted the meaning of Bank Notes in Section 2(aiv) of the RBI Act, 1934. It means a bank note issued by the RBI, whether in physical or digital form, under Section 22 of the RBI Act, 1934.

Central Bank Digital Currency (CBDC) and its Classification:

In a significant move, the government has expanded the definition of bank notes to encompass not only physical currency but also those issued in digital form.

This strategic inclusion directly positions **Central Bank Digital Currency (CBDC)** within the scope of bank notes, and consequently, as Indian currency.

Key Implication: By classifying CBDC as Indian currency, it is explicitly excluded from being categorized as a Virtual Digital Asset (VDA). This distinction carries substantial implications for the taxation and regulatory treatment of CBDC.

Rationale and Potential Benefits:

This move aligns with the government's broader strategy to promote the adoption and use of CBDC as a legitimate and recognized form of currency. By clarifying its legal status and differentiating it from speculative digital assets, the government aims to foster trust and confidence in CBDC.

Potential benefits of this classification include:

- **Simplified Taxation:** Treating CBDC as currency could lead to a more straightforward tax regime compared to the complex and evolving tax treatment of VDAs.

- **Regulatory Clarity:** Explicitly defining CBDC's legal status provides regulatory clarity for financial institutions, businesses, and individuals dealing with CBDC.

- **Enhanced Adoption:** The classification may encourage wider adoption of CBDC by businesses and consumers, as it reduces uncertainty and aligns CBDC with existing legal and financial frameworks.

Future Outlook:

The inclusion of CBDC within the definition of bank notes represents a significant step in India's digital currency landscape. It paves the way for the potential rollout of CBDC and provides a regulatory framework that balances innovation with stability. As the CBDC ecosystem evolves, further regulations and guidelines are expected to be introduced to address specific operational, security, and privacy aspects.

A Central Bank Digital Currency (CBDC) is a digital version of a country's national currency, issued and backed by the country's central bank. It is equivalent to the physical currency and can be exchanged on a one-to-one basis with the physical currency. CBDCs are currently being explored and tested by various central banks around the world but are not yet fully implemented in most countries.

A CBDC is denominated in the same currency as the country that issues it and holds the same value as the physical currency. For example, a digital dollar issued by the US Federal Reserve would be a CBDC and would hold the same value as a physical dollar bill.

The key difference between CBDCs and cryptocurrencies like Bitcoin is that CBDCs are centralized and controlled by the central bank, while cryptocurrencies are decentralized and operate on a blockchain network. CBDCs aim to provide the benefits of digital currencies, such as faster and cheaper transactions, while maintaining the stability and security of a national currency.

Foreign Currency and Virtual Digital Assets:

Under Section 2(m) of the Foreign Exchange Management Act (FEMA) 1999, foreign currency is defined as any currency other than Indian currency. This includes the official currency of every foreign country, regardless of whether it is prohibited for remittance. Therefore, all foreign currencies are excluded from the definition of a Virtual Digital Asset (VDA).

Cryptocurrencies as Legal Tender:

An interesting question arises with countries like El Salvador and the Central African Republic adopting Bitcoin as legal tender and an official currency. Does this mean Bitcoin is considered a foreign currency in these jurisdictions and therefore not a VDA?

Potential Implications:

If Bitcoin is considered a foreign currency in countries where it is legal tender, it could have significant implications for taxation and regulation. It might be treated similarly to traditional foreign currencies for purposes of exchange control, remittance, and reporting. However, this could also create complexities and challenges for cross-border transactions and regulatory harmonization.

Need for Clarity:

The evolving landscape of cryptocurrencies and their adoption as legal tender raises questions about the existing legal and regulatory frameworks. There is a need for clear guidelines and definitions to address the classification and treatment of cryptocurrencies in different jurisdictions, especially in cases where they are recognized as official currencies.

Cryptocurrencies exist in a decentralized digital realm, transcending national borders and eluding traditional classification systems. Unlike fiat currencies, which are issued and regulated by specific countries, cryptocurrencies lack inherent attributes that tie them to a particular jurisdiction. They are not bound by geographical boundaries or subject to the control of any single government.

This borderless nature of cryptocurrencies poses challenges for regulators and tax authorities seeking to enforce compliance and impose jurisdictional controls. As cryptocurrencies flow seamlessly across borders, it becomes increasingly difficult to track their origins, ownership, and transactional history. The absence of clear jurisdictional boundaries raises questions about which country has the authority to tax cryptocurrency transactions and how to prevent tax evasion and money laundering.

Moreover, the pseudonymous nature of many cryptocurrency transactions further complicates efforts to identify and trace the movement of funds. While blockchain technology provides a transparent and immutable record of transactions, the identities of the parties involved are often obscured by cryptographic keys and pseudonyms. This anonymity makes it challenging for authorities to attribute cryptocurrency holdings to specific individuals or entities, and to determine their tax liabilities.

"Foreign currency" is defined to mean any currency other than Indian currency. Thus, foreign currency must also be a currency. 'Currency' is defined under section 2(h) of the FEMA 1999 to include all currency notes, postal notes, postal orders, money orders, cheques, drafts, travellers cheques, letters of credit, bills of exchange and promissory notes, credit cards or such other similar instruments, as may be notified by the RBI. The virtual digital asset is not covered under the definition of currency. Thus, it cannot be regarded as foreign currency. Hence, even if El Salvador announced the Bitcoin as its official currency, the Bitcoin cannot be treated as foreign currency because it does not fall in the definition of currency itself.

TAX ON INCOME ARISING FROM TRANSFER OF VIRTUAL DIGITAL ASSET

The Finance Act, 2022 has inserted a new Section 115BBH to tax the income arising from transfer of virtual digital assets. The Section 115BBH reads as:

1. Where the total income of an assessee includes any income from the transfer of any virtual digital asset, notwithstanding anything contained in any other provision of this Act, the income-tax payable shall be the aggregate of–

    •   the amount of income-tax calculated on the income from transfer of such virtual digital asset at the rate of thirty per cent; and

    •   the amount of income-tax with which the assessee would have been chargeable, had the total income of the assessee been reduced by the income referred to in clause (a).

2. Notwithstanding anything contained in any other provision of this Act,–

    •   no deduction in respect of any expenditure (other than cost of acquisition, if any) or allowance or set of of any loss shall be allowed to the assessee under any provision of this Act in computing the income referred to in clause (a) of sub-section (1); and

- no set of of loss from transfer of the virtual digital asset computed under clause (a) of sub- section (1) shall be allowed against income computed under any provision of this Act to the assessee and such loss shall not be allowed to be carried forward to succeeding assessment years.

3. For the purposes of this section, the word "transfer" as defined in clause (47) of section 2, shall apply to any virtual digital asset, whether capital asset or not.

The tax on VDA under section 115BBH is as:

Key Points and Elaboration on Taxation of Virtual Digital Assets (VDAs) in India:

1. **Transfer of VDA and Tax Implication:**

    - **Scope of Transfer:** Any transfer of a Virtual Digital Asset (VDA), irrespective of whether it is held as a capital asset (long-term investment) or a trading asset (short-term investment), is subject to taxation.

This encompasses various transactions like selling, exchanging, or gifting VDAs.

- **Income Generation:** The transfer of a VDA must result in income to be taxable. If the transfer results in a loss, it is disregarded for tax purposes and cannot be claimed as a deduction.

2. **Tax Rate and Calculation:**

- **Flat Tax Rate:** Income from the transfer of VDAs is taxed at a flat rate of 30%. This rate is applicable regardless of the individual's income tax bracket or slab rate.

- **No Basic Exemption:** The basic exemption limit, which is available for other sources of income, does not apply to income from VDA transfers.

- **Deductions:** The only deduction allowed when calculating taxable income from VDA transfers is the cost of acquisition of the VDA. Expenses like brokerage, commission, and other transfer-related costs are not deductible.

3. **Loss Set-off and Carry Forward:**

- **No Loss Set-off:** Losses incurred from the transfer of one VDA cannot be set off against income from the transfer of another VDA or against any other income source.

- **No Carry Forward:** Losses from VDA transfers cannot be carried forward to future assessment years to offset against future income. These losses are essentially dead losses and cannot be utilized for tax purposes in any way.

Key Implication: The tax treatment of VDAs in India is stringent. The flat tax rate, absence of basic exemption, and restrictions on loss set-off and carry forward highlight the government's focus on revenue generation from VDA transactions. It is crucial for investors and traders to be aware of these tax implications and factor them into their financial planning.

Chargeability of VDA:

The income arising from transfer of VDA shall be chargeable to tax as per provisions of the law, i.e.,

- section 4 (charge of income tax)

- section 5 (scope of total income)

- section 9 (income deemed to accrue or arise in India)

- section 14 (heads of income) of the Income-tax Act, 1961

VDA TAXATION FOR NRI

Taxation in India: Residence and Source-Based Principles:

India's taxation system operates on two fundamental principles: the residence of the taxpayer and the source of income. These principles determine the scope of income subject to taxation in India.

Residence-Based Taxation:

Indian residents are subject to taxation on their global income. This means that all income earned by an Indian resident, whether within India or abroad, is liable to be taxed in India.

Source-Based Taxation:

Non-residents, on the other hand, are subject to source-based taxation. This implies that only income that is received or accrued from a source in India, or deemed to accrue or arise in India, is subject to income tax in India. Section 9 of the Income Tax Act, 1961, provides specific provisions outlining the circumstances under which certain income is deemed to accrue or arise in India, and therefore becomes taxable for non-residents.

Key Points:

- The residence status of the taxpayer (resident or non-resident) is crucial in determining the scope of income subject to taxation.

- Indian residents are taxed on their worldwide income, while non-residents are taxed only on income sourced in India.

- The concept of deemed accrual or arising of income in India extends the tax net to certain income earned by non-residents, ensuring that income with a substantial Indian connection is not exempt from taxation.

SITUS OF VDA

In the realm of cryptocurrency taxation, determining the tax liability for non-residents on gains from the transfer of Virtual Digital Assets (VDAs) hinges significantly on establishing the VDA's situs or place of origin.

If the situs of a VDA is determined to be within India, any income accruing to a non-resident from the transfer of that VDA will be subject to taxation in India. This taxation will be governed by the provisions outlined in Section 9(1)(i) of the Income Tax Act and the stipulations of the relevant Double Taxation Avoidance Agreement (DTAA).

Therefore, understanding the concept of situs and its application in the context of VDAs is crucial for non-residents involved in VDA transactions in India. The determination of situs can be a complex process, potentially involving factors such as the location of the VDA's underlying assets, the residence of the parties involved in the transaction, and the place where the transfer is executed.

It is also important to note that the provisions of the relevant DTAA can significantly impact the tax liability of a non-resident. DTAs are bilateral agreements between countries that aim to avoid double taxation of income. They often contain specific provisions relating to the taxation of VDAs, which may override the general provisions of domestic tax law.

In conclusion, the taxation of VDAs for non-residents in India is a multifaceted issue with significant implications. Non-residents engaging in VDA transactions in India need to be aware of the potential tax liabilities and seek professional advice to ensure compliance with the relevant tax laws.

The situs/location of an asset needs to be checked only for non-resident assessees and not ordinarily resident assessees (global income of ordinary residents is taxable in India). In the cases of non-resident assessees, if an asset, located outside India, is transferred outside India and sale proceeds are received outside India, no taxability arises in view of section 5 of the Act [except in case of shares/interest as referred to in Explanation 5 to Section 9(1)(i)]. Such assessees will be liable to be taxed under section 9(1)(i) of the Act in respect of income accruing or arising through the transfer of any property, asset or capital asset situated in India. Explanation 5 states that "For the removal of doubts, it is hereby clarified that an asset or a capital asset being any share or interest in a company or entity registered or incorporated outside India shall be deemed to be and shall always be deemed to have been situated in India, if the share or interest derives, directly or indirectly, its value substantially from the assets located in India."

In the current legal framework, the Income-tax Act lacks explicit provisions to ascertain the situs (or location) of Virtual Digital Assets (VDAs). Given the intangible nature of VDAs, it becomes imperative to rely on judicial pronouncements that have addressed the situs of intangible property to determine the location of VDAs. This approach acknowledges the unique characteristics of VDAs and seeks to apply existing legal principles to this emerging asset class.

By examining judicial precedents related to intangible property, legal practitioners and tax authorities can gain valuable insights into the factors that courts consider when determining the situs of such assets. These factors may include the residence or domicile of the owner, the location of the servers or platforms where the VDAs are stored or traded, and the place where the economic activity associated with the VDAs occurs.

It is crucial to recognize that the determination of the situs of VDAs has significant implications for taxation purposes. The jurisdiction in which a VDA is deemed to be located may have the right to tax the income or gains arising from the VDA. Therefore, a clear and consistent approach to determining the situs of VDAs is essential to ensure legal certainty and prevent double taxation.

As the legal and regulatory landscape surrounding VDAs continues to evolve, it is possible that specific provisions regarding the situs of VDAs may be introduced in the Income-tax Act or other relevant legislation. However, until such provisions are enacted, the reliance on judicial pronouncements and the principles established therein remains the most viable approach to determining the situs of VDAs.

In the case of CUB Pty Ltd. v. Union of India [2016] 71 taxmann.com 315/241 Taxman 278 (Delhi), the Delhi High Court held as under:

"(b) An intangible asset, by its very nature, does not have any physical form. Therefore, it does not exist in a physical form at any particular location. The legislature could have, through a deeming fiction, provided for the location of an intangible asset but, it has not done so insofar. With regard to a share or interest in a company registered/incorporated outside India, Explanation 5 has been added to section 9(1)(i) by virtue of the Finance Act, 2012 with retrospective effect from 1-4-1962.

(c) Thus, the legislature, where it wanted to specifically provide for a particular situation, as in the case of shares, where the share derives, directly or indirectly, its value substantially from assets located in India, it did

so. There is no such provision with regard to intangible assets. Therefore, the well accepted principle of 'mobilia sequuntur personam' would have to be followed. The situs of the owner of an intangible asset would be the closest approximation of the situs of an intangible asset. This is an internationally accepted rule, unless it is altered by local legislation. There is no such alteration in the Indian context."

Expanding on the Notion of Situs for Virtual Digital Assets (VDAs):

Determining the situs, or location, of a Virtual Digital Asset (VDA) for taxation purposes is a complex issue with multiple potential approaches. While factors like the user's residence or the location of the exchange play a role, another perspective suggests that the **physical location of the servers where the VDA is stored** could also be a determining factor in establishing situs.

This viewpoint stems from the idea that the VDA, while intangible, is ultimately represented by data stored on physical servers. These servers have a tangible location, and that location could be argued to have a bearing on the VDA's situs. This approach aligns with the traditional concept of situs for physical assets, where the location of the asset itself is a primary factor in determining jurisdiction for taxation.

However, this approach also presents challenges. VDAs can be stored across multiple servers in different locations, making it difficult to pinpoint a single situs. Additionally, the location of servers can be easily changed, potentially leading to ambiguity and disputes over jurisdiction.

Despite these challenges, the location of servers where VDAs are stored remains a relevant consideration in the ongoing debate over situs determination for VDAs. As technology continues to evolve and VDAs become increasingly prevalent, it is likely that this perspective will continue to be explored and debated by tax authorities and legal experts around the world.

If there are several criteria on the basis of which situs of intangible property can be decided and there is no definite criteria which would attribute situs to India, the courts / tribunals would always be in favour of the taxpayer. It has already been held in Vodafone International Holdings B.V. v. Union of India [2008] 175 Taxman 399 (Bom.) and Azadi Bachao Andolan's case (supra) that if the owner of the property is not a resident of India and property is transferred outside India then income arising on its transfer cannot be taxed in India. Explanation 5 to section 9(1)(i) alters the situation only to a limited extent in case of shares and interest in a company and their locations will be deemed to be in India if substantial assets of the company are in India. In case of other intangible assets, there are no such provisions in the Income-tax Act. Therefore, even if intangible assets are developed, used or commercially exploited in India, still income arising from their transfer outside India cannot be taxed in India. It would clearly be a case of profit shifting. Therefore, if leakage of revenue is sought to be plugged, amendment has to be brought in the Act on the similar lines to Explanation 5 to Section 9(1)(i) specifically for intangible assets.

In the absence of specific provisions within the Act, determining the situs of intangible property relies heavily on the domicile of the owner. If the owner of the intangible asset is not a resident of India, any income generated from the transfer of that asset outside of India cannot be taxed within India. This principle stems from the understanding that a country's taxing authority generally extends only to its residents and to activities occurring within its borders.

Therefore, if the government aims to prevent the potential loss of tax revenue due to the transfer of intangible assets by non-residents outside India, it would be necessary to amend the existing laws. Specifically, expanding the scope of Explanation 5 to encompass other intangible assets would be a crucial step. This amendment would allow the Indian government to assert its taxing authority over a wider range of intangible assets, even when owned by non-residents, potentially preventing the shifting of revenue outside its jurisdiction.

However, such an amendment must be carefully crafted to ensure it aligns with international tax norms and does not create undue burdens or deter foreign investment. It is a delicate balancing act between protecting the country's tax base and maintaining a favorable environment for global economic engagement.

CLASSIFICATION OF VDA

The income generated from the transfer of Virtual Digital Assets (VDAs) can fall under different categories within the Indian Income Tax framework. These categories determine the applicable tax rates and the manner in which the income is treated for tax purposes:

- **Profits and Gains from Business or Profession (PGBP):** This category applies if the taxpayer's activities involving VDAs constitute a business or profession. Factors such as the frequency of transactions, the intention to make a profit, the systematic and organized nature of operations, and the volume of transactions are considered when determining whether VDA transactions are classified as business income. If classified under PGBP, the income is taxed according to the applicable slab rates for business income, and expenses incurred in connection with the business can be deducted.

- **Income under the Head of Capital Gains:** This category applies if the VDAs are considered capital assets in the hands of the taxpayer. The tax treatment will depend on whether the gains are short-term or long-term. Short-term capital gains are taxed as per the taxpayer's ordinary income tax slab rates, while long-term capital gains are taxed at a specified rate. The period for which the VDA is held determines whether the gains are short-term or long-term.

- **Income from Other Sources:** This is a residuary category that applies when the income from VDA transfers does not fall under any other specific head of income. Income classified under this head is taxed at the applicable slab rates.

It is crucial to accurately classify the income from VDA transfers under the appropriate head to ensure compliance with tax regulations and avoid penalties. The specific circumstances of each taxpayer and the nature of their VDA transactions will determine the correct classification. Consulting with a qualified tax professional is advisable to ensure proper tax treatment of VDA-related income.

Taxable under the head of PGBP – When an entity buy VDA for sale in the ordinary course of business as trading activity, the profits arising therefrom is taxed under the head PGBP. This would apply in particular to traders/dealers of cryptocurrencies. Whereas, if the VDAs are held as a capital asset, the income shall be taxed under the head "capital gain". When an asset should be treated as a capital asset or a trading asset is an issue that has led to a lot of litigation especially in the case of shares and securities. To reduce litigation and maintain consistency in approach, the CBDT had issued various circulars prescribing the principles to classify shares or securities as capital asset or trading asset [See, Instruction No. 1827, dated 31-8-1989, Circular No. 4, dated 15-6-2017 and Circular No. 6, dated 29-2-2016]. Though the aforesaid instruction and circulars are applicable in the case of securities, the principles prescribed therein can be applied to classify VDAs as a capital asset or trading asset. Though, these instructions and circulars were prominently for shares and securities not for VDAs.

Taxable under the head of Capital Gains – As per Section 2(14), 'capital asset' means property of any kind held by an assessee, whether or not connected with his business or profession. The word 'property' is of the widest amplitude, including the right and interest of a person in a particular asset. Every possible interest that a person can hold or enjoy in an asset can be termed as 'property' within the definition of a capital asset. Any right which can be called property is included in the definition of 'capital assets'. It would comprise a bundle of rights and interests that a person may conceivably hold and enjoy. It includes such rights that a person may lawfully exercise to the exclusion of others or entitled to use and enjoy as he pleases, provided he does not infringe any law of the State. It is also defined as an aggregate of rights having monetary value. It includes money and all other property, real or personal, including things in action and other intangible property.

A VDA possesses all elements a capital asset has. Thus, if the VDAs are not held as stock-in-trade in the books of account or the assessee is not engaged in the business of dealing in VDAs, the resultant gains should be taxable under the head of the capital gains.

Though the tax rates are the same and notwithstanding the income is taxed under the head of business or profession, capital gains or other sources.

Taxable under the head of other sources – As per Section 56(1), any income shall be chargeable to tax under the head "Income from other sources", if it is not chargeable under any other heads. Therefore, the classification of such income should be tested first under the head of business income or capital gains. Head of income from other sources is a residuary head of income. If income does not fall in another head of income then it is covered under the head of income from other sources. Only on unsuccessful classification, under another head of income, it can be taxed under the head of other sources [see CIT v. Smt. T.P. Sidhwa [1981] 6 Taxman 91/[1982] 133 ITR 840 (Bom.)].

Importance of Sec 234C in classification of VDA:

The categorization of Virtual Digital Assets (VDAs) into business income, capital gains, or other sources of income is a crucial step in determining the interest payable under Section 234C of the Income Tax Act. This section deals with the interest levied on taxpayers for failing to pay advance tax on their income.

A significant provision within Section 234C is the exemption of interest on delayed advance tax payments for income classified as capital gains. This means that if a taxpayer underestimates or fails to estimate the accrual of capital gains, leading to a shortfall in advance tax payment, they will not be liable to pay interest under Section 234C.

However, this exemption does not extend to other categories of income. If the shortfall in advance tax payment is due to underestimation or non-estimation of business income or income from other sources, interest will be payable under Section 234C.

Therefore, accurate classification of VDA income is essential not only for tax computation but also for determining interest liability on delayed advance tax payments. Taxpayers and their advisors need to exercise due diligence in classifying VDA income to ensure compliance with tax laws and avoid unnecessary interest charges.

TRANSFER OF VDA

Section 115BBH of the Income Tax Act in India, which governs the taxation of Virtual Digital Assets (VDAs), specifies that the definition of "transfer" will be applicable to all VDAs, regardless of whether they are classified as capital assets or not. This means that any income generated from VDAs will be calculated and taxed according to the provisions of Section 115BBH, irrespective of whether it falls under the category of business or profession, capital gains, or other sources of income.

In essence, this provision ensures that all income derived from VDAs is subject to taxation under Section 115BBH, thereby eliminating any ambiguity regarding the tax treatment of such income. This approach aims to create a uniform and comprehensive tax regime for VDAs, ensuring that all income generated from these assets is brought within the tax net.

Transfers Not Chargeable to Tax:

Exemptions from Taxation under Section 115BBH for Virtual Digital Assets (VDAs):

While Section 115BBH of the Income Tax Act imposes a 30% tax on profits from the transfer of VDAs, certain transactions are exempt from this tax provision. These exemptions include:

- **Lending of virtual digital assets:** Interest earned from lending VDAs is not considered taxable income under Section 115BBH. This exemption encourages the utilization of VDAs in decentralized finance (DeFi) protocols and lending platforms.

- **Distribution of assets in kind during liquidation:** When a company undergoes liquidation and distributes VDAs to its shareholders as part of the liquidation process, this distribution is not treated as a taxable transfer by the company. However, shareholders may be liable to pay tax on any capital gains arising from the receipt of these VDAs. This exemption ensures that companies are not penalized for distributing assets to shareholders during liquidation.

- **Transfers specified in Section 47:** Transfers of VDAs that fall under Section 47 of the Income Tax Act are exempt from taxation under Section 115BBH. These transfers include gifts, transfers through a will or inheritance, partition of a Hindu Undivided Family (HUF), and business restructuring transactions. This exemption recognizes that these transfers are not typically undertaken for profit-making purposes and should not be subject to the 30% tax rate.

It is important to note that while these transactions are exempt from taxation under Section 115BBH, they may still be subject to other tax provisions. For example, capital gains arising from the receipt of VDAs during liquidation may be taxable under the general capital gains tax regime.

Transfer by way of conversion into stock-in-trade:

Let's delve deeper into the tax implications when a cryptocurrency asset transitions from an investment to a business asset.

Conversion from Investment to Stock-in-Trade:

When a cryptocurrency, initially acquired as an investment, is later converted into stock-in-trade for a business operation, the tax laws consider this conversion as a taxable event. The cryptocurrency is deemed to have been transferred in the financial year in which this conversion took place. Consequently, a capital gain is calculated and recorded for that specific year.

Taxation Year:

While the capital gain is calculated in the year of conversion, the tax liability on this gain is deferred. The tax payment becomes due in the year when the stock-in-trade (the cryptocurrency that was converted) is eventually sold or transferred by the taxpayer.

Dual Taxation:

In the year that the stock-in-trade is sold, two distinct types of income become taxable:

- **Capital Gains:** The capital gain that was calculated at the time of converting the cryptocurrency from an investment to a business asset. This is taxed under the 'capital gains' category.

- **Business Income:** The profit generated from the sale of the stock-in-trade (the cryptocurrency). This is taxed under the 'profits and gains of business or profession' category.

Key Point: The conversion of a cryptocurrency from an investment to a business asset triggers a taxable event, even though the tax payment is deferred. This approach ensures that both the capital appreciation during the investment phase and the business profit from the sale are subject to taxation.

Example: Mr. X acquired bitcoins worth Rs. 5 lakh as investments on 4th April 2023 then Mr. X launched one trading platform and converted this investment into stock-in-trade on 28th December 2023 on this date value of these bitcoins is Rs. 6.2 lakhs. He sold these bitcoins as stock-in-trade amounting to Rs. 7.6 lakhs in FY 2024-25.

Solution: It is deemed that bitcoin (as capital asset) transferred in FY 2023-24. Capital gain arising on this becomes payable in the year in which such capital asset converted into stock is sold i.e in FY 2024-25. During FY 2024–25 tax on capital gain of Rs. 1.2 lakh (6.2–5 lakh) and business income of Rs. 1.4 lakh (7.6–6.2 lakh) is payable.

Similarly, if VDAs held as inventory of a business are converted into capital assets, its fair market value as on the date of its conversion shall be taxable as business income under Section 28(via).

Example: Mr. X acquired bitcoins worth Rs. 5 lakh as stock-in-trade on 4th April 2023. During FY 2024-25 on 8th May 2024 this stock in trade converted into capital assets, on this date FMV of these bitcoins is Rs. 7.6 lakh.

Solution: In FY 2024-25 Rs. 2.6 lakh (7.6–5 lakh) is taxable as business income.

LENDING OF CRYPTOCURRENCIES

Within the cryptocurrency landscape, numerous exchanges provide investors with the opportunity to lend their cryptocurrency holdings and earn interest. This lending activity is distinct from a transfer or sale, as the title or ownership of the asset does not pass to the borrower. It is simply a loan agreement where the cryptocurrency is temporarily lent in exchange for interest payments.

The interest earned from lending cryptocurrency is typically credited to the investor in the same cryptocurrency that was lent. This interest income should be classified and taxed under the head 'Income from other sources' for individuals or 'Profits and Gains from Business or Profession (PGBP)' for businesses, depending on the nature of the investor's activities. The applicable tax rate for this income would be the standard rate for the investor's income bracket, and not the special rate of 30% specified under Section 115BBH of the Income Tax Act.

Section 115BBH deals specifically with income from the transfer of Virtual Digital Assets (VDA), and since interest income from lending VDA does not involve a transfer of ownership, it does not fall under the purview of this section. Therefore, it is taxed at the normal applicable rates.

It is important for investors to understand the tax implications of lending their cryptocurrency holdings. By recognizing that interest income from lending is taxed differently than income from the sale of cryptocurrency, investors can ensure they are compliant with tax regulations and avoid any potential penalties.

Can a person engaged in lending of VDAs claim depreciation on it as intangible asset?

Section 32 of the Income Tax Act allows for depreciation on intangible assets, which include know-how, patents, copyrights, trademarks, licenses, franchises, and other similar business or commercial rights. The interpretation of the phrase "any other business or commercial rights of similar nature" has been clarified by court rulings to encompass rights that are either similar to the explicitly listed categories or fall within the same origin.

A Virtual Digital Asset (VDA) does not share characteristics with the specified intangible assets and does not originate from the same source. Therefore, it cannot be classified as an intangible asset for the purpose of claiming depreciation under Section 32.

TAX ON MINING OF VDA

When an individual engages in cryptocurrency mining by utilizing their computational resources to solve intricate mathematical problems, they are rewarded with newly minted cryptocurrency tokens and transaction fees for their contribution to the network. The creation of new cryptocurrency units through mining can be considered a taxable event, particularly when the miner receives these units. In most tax jurisdictions, the receipt of mined cryptocurrency is viewed as the initial taxable event. However, a considerable number of countries have also indicated that tax liability doesn't arise until the disposal or sale of the mined cryptocurrency.

In the context of India's tax laws, Section 56(2)(vi) of the Income Tax Act, which taxes any sum of money exceeding Rs. 50,000 received without consideration by an individual or Hindu Undivided Family (HUF), might not be applicable to mined cryptocurrency. This is because Virtual Digital Assets (VDAs) may not be classified as "any sum of money."

However, when the mined VDA is eventually sold or disposed of, it becomes taxable under the provisions of Section 115BBH of the Income Tax Act. This section deals specifically with the taxation of income from the transfer of VDAs. The tax rate and other relevant provisions for the taxation of VDAs are outlined in this section.

Therefore, while the receipt of mined cryptocurrency may not trigger immediate tax liability in certain jurisdictions, including India, the subsequent sale or disposal of such cryptocurrency is subject to taxation as per the applicable tax laws. It is crucial for cryptocurrency miners to be aware of the tax implications associated with their mining activities and to ensure compliance with the relevant tax regulations.

In India, the taxation of cryptocurrency transactions is centered around the concept of 'disposal' rather than 'mining'. While mining cryptocurrency can be seen as the creation of an asset, it doesn't inherently involve the transfer of ownership. Therefore, mining cryptocurrency itself doesn't trigger a taxable event in India.

The tax liability, as outlined in Section 115BBH of the Income Tax Act, arises only when the mined cryptocurrency is eventually transferred or sold. This transfer event is when the income is realized and becomes taxable.

Furthermore, Section 56(2)(x) of the Income Tax Act, which deals with income from other sources, is not applicable to cryptocurrency received through mining. This section is relevant only when the asset is received "from a person". Since mining doesn't involve receiving cryptocurrency from another individual or entity, it falls outside the purview of this section.

Therefore, the current tax framework in India focuses on the actual transfer or sale of cryptocurrency as the taxable event, while the mining activity itself remains exempt from taxation until that point.

Transfer without consideration:

The transfer of Virtual Digital Assets (VDAs) can occur in various scenarios:

- **For Consideration:** This involves the exchange of a VDA for fiat currency, another virtual currency or digital asset, or for a good or service. In such cases, the transfer is subject to taxation under Section 115BBH of the Income Tax Act.

- **Without Consideration:** This includes transfers made without a reciprocal exchange of value, such as gifts or inheritances.

  - **Impact on Transferor:** The transfer is tax-neutral for the person transferring the VDA.

  - **Impact on Recipient:** The recipient of the VDA is liable to pay tax under either Section 56(2)(x) or Section 28(iv), depending on the specific circumstances.

It is important to note that the Finance Act, 2022 introduced a significant amendment by including virtual digital assets within the definition of 'property' for the purpose of Section 56(2)(x). This amendment has implications for the taxation of VDAs received as gifts.

Transfer by way of donation of VDAs:

Donations of Virtual Digital Assets (VDAs) to Charitable or Religious Trusts

Tax Implications for the Donor:

When an individual donates VDAs (e.g., cryptocurrencies) to a charitable or religious trust or institution, it is not considered a taxable transfer. This means the donor does not incur tax liability on the donation. However, the donor also cannot claim a tax deduction under Section 80G for the donation, as it is made in kind (i.e., not in cash).

Tax Implications for the Recipient Trust:

The recipient trust is generally not taxed on the value of the donated VDA, provided certain conditions are met:

1.   **Corpus Donations:**

- If the VDA donation is specifically designated to become part of the trust's corpus (i.e., its permanent funds), it is exempt from tax.

- However, this exemption is subject to the condition that the donation is invested or deposited in specific forms or modes as outlined in Section 11(5) of the Income Tax Act, and these investments or deposits are maintained specifically for the corpus.

2.   **Non-Corpus Donations:**

- If the VDA donation is not part of the corpus, it must be used for charitable or religious purposes in India to be exempt from tax.

- If at least 85% of the donation is not used for charitable purposes in the previous year, it must be accumulated and used for religious or charitable purposes within the next 5 years.

Investment and Accumulation Requirements:

Both the exemption for corpus donations and the accumulation of funds for 5 years are contingent upon the contributions being invested or deposited in specific forms or modes as specified in Section 11(5) of the Income Tax Act. These investments or deposits must be maintained specifically for the corpus or the accumulated funds.

Key Points:

- Donating VDAs to charitable or religious trusts is not a taxable event for the donor.

- The recipient trust is generally exempt from tax on VDA donations, provided they meet specific conditions regarding corpus integration, charitable use, and investment or deposit of the funds.

- Understanding these tax implications is crucial for both donors and recipient trusts when dealing with VDA donations.

VDAs LOST OR STOLEN

The loss or theft of virtual digital assets is a significant risk. Cryptocurrencies, for instance, can be irretrievably lost due to a variety of reasons. One common scenario is the misplacement or forgetting of the private key that grants access to a cryptocurrency wallet. Without this key, the assets held within the wallet become inaccessible. Another scenario where loss can occur is upon inheritance, if the deceased owner did not share the private key or provide access to the wallet in any other way. This could result in the inheritor being unable to claim the digital assets, effectively losing them.

The risk of theft is also prevalent in the realm of cryptocurrencies. Hackers and cybercriminals are constantly devising new ways to infiltrate cryptocurrency wallets and exchanges to steal digital assets. Additionally, phishing scams and other fraudulent schemes can trick individuals into divulging their private keys or other sensitive information, leading to the theft of their cryptocurrencies.

Therefore, it is crucial for individuals who own virtual digital assets to take adequate security measures to protect their investments. This includes safeguarding private keys, using secure wallets, and being vigilant against potential scams and cyberattacks.

In the Indian context, the tax implications surrounding the loss or theft of Virtual Digital Assets (VDAs) have been a subject of debate. A significant legal precedent was set by the Supreme Court in the case of Vania Silk Mills (P.) Ltd. v. CIT 59 Taxman 3 (SC). The court held that the destruction of an asset doesn't constitute a transfer, as the asset must exist for a transfer to occur.

This ruling has implications for VDAs that are stolen or lost. Since these situations don't fall under the definition of a transfer, they aren't governed by the specific tax provisions for transfers, such as Section 115BBH of the Income Tax Act. Instead, the tax treatment in these cases would be determined by the general provisions of the Income Tax Act.

Furthermore, if the VDAs were considered capital assets by the owner, the loss due to theft or misplacement wouldn't be recognized as a capital loss. This distinction is crucial, as it prevents the owner from claiming a deduction for the lost value of the VDAs against their capital gains.

This legal position creates a challenging situation for VDA owners. While the loss of VDAs due to theft or misplacement represents a real financial loss, the current tax framework doesn't allow for this loss to be recognized for tax purposes.

Transfer of VDA by employer to employee:

Tax Implications of Virtual Digital Assets (VDAs) Provided by Employers to Employees

1. **VDAs as Remuneration:**

   When an employer gives VDAs to an employee as part of their salary or compensation package, the value of these VDAs is considered a taxable perquisite in the hands of the employee. This falls under Section 17(2)(iii) of the Income Tax Act. The value of the VDA is determined based on its fair market value at the time it is given to the employee.

2. **VDAs as Gifts:**

   There is an exception to the taxation rule if the VDAs are given as a gift by the employer to the employee or their family members on special occasions like festivals, birthdays, or other celebrations. In this case, the VDAs are not considered taxable if the total value of all gifts received during the financial year is less than or equal to Rs. 5,000. However, if the total value of gifts exceeds Rs. 5,000, the entire value of the gifts becomes taxable as a perquisite in the hands of the employee.

3. **Tax Liability for the Employer:**

    When an employer transfers VDAs to employees, the employer is also liable to pay tax on the income generated from this transfer. This income is calculated as the difference between the fair market value of the VDA on the date of transfer and the cost of acquiring the VDA. This income is taxed under Section 115BBH of the Income Tax Act.

Key Points to Remember:

- VDAs given as salary are taxable as perquisites for employees.

- VDAs given as gifts are taxable only if the total value of gifts exceeds Rs. 5,000 in a financial year.

- Employers are liable to pay tax on the income generated from transferring VDAs to employees.

- The fair market value of the VDA is crucial in determining the tax liability for both employees and employers.

COMPUTATION OF INCOME TAXABLE UNDER SECTION 115BBH

The income arising from transfer of virtual digital assets shall be computed in the following manner:

Particulars	Amount
Full value of consideration	xxx
Less: Cost of acquisition, if any	(xxx)
Income from VDA	xxx

Section 115BBH(2)(a) of the Income Tax Act, 1961, lays down a crucial provision concerning the taxation of virtual digital assets (VDAs) in India. It explicitly states that when computing the income from the transfer of VDAs, no deduction is permissible in respect of any expenditure incurred, other than the cost of acquisition, if any. Furthermore, it disallows any allowance or set-off of any loss.

In simpler terms, this provision implies that while calculating the taxable income from VDA transactions, taxpayers cannot claim deductions for any expenses they might have incurred, except for the cost they initially paid to acquire the VDA. Additionally, any losses incurred in VDA transactions cannot be used to offset against other income or gains.

This provision has significant implications for taxpayers involved in VDA transactions. For instance, it means that expenses such as commission, platform fees, or brokerage paid during the purchase or sale of VDAs cannot be deducted from the taxable income. Similarly, any loss incurred due to a decrease in the value of VDAs cannot be set off against other income.

EXCHANGE OF VDA

In the context of cryptocurrency transactions on an exchange platform, when one Virtual Digital Asset (VDA) is exchanged for another VDA, or the consideration for the transaction is received in the form of another VDA, the fair market value of the VDA received will be considered as the full value of the consideration for the transaction. This is in line with the general principle of valuing assets at their fair market value for taxation purposes.

However, there may be situations where determining the fair market value of the VDA received as consideration is not possible or cannot be ascertained with certainty. In such scenarios, the tax laws provide a fallback provision. According to Section 50D of the Income Tax Act, 1961, if the fair market value of the consideration received cannot be determined, the fair market value of the VDA that was transferred or given up in the exchange will be deemed to be the full value of the consideration. This ensures that even in cases where the value of the consideration is uncertain, the transaction can still be valued for tax purposes, and the taxpayer can be held accountable for the appropriate tax liability.

Section 115BBH of the Income Tax Act, which governs the taxation of virtual digital assets, presents ambiguity in its application due to the lack of a clearly defined method for determining the fair market value of these assets. Unlike other sections of the Act, such as Section 50CA and Section 50B, Section 115BBH does not provide a specific formula for calculating fair market value, nor does it authorize the Central Board of Direct Taxes (CBDT) to prescribe one. This absence of explicit guidelines creates uncertainty and potential inconsistencies in the valuation of virtual digital assets for tax purposes.

The lack of specific rules or methodologies for determining fair market value can lead to challenges in both tax compliance and enforcement. Taxpayers may struggle to accurately assess the value of their virtual digital assets, potentially leading to underreporting or overreporting of income. Additionally, the absence of a standardized valuation method can create difficulties for tax authorities in verifying the accuracy of reported values and enforcing tax laws. This ambiguity may also increase the potential for disputes between taxpayers and tax authorities regarding the fair market value of virtual digital assets.

To address these issues, it is crucial to establish clear guidelines and methodologies for determining the fair market value of virtual digital assets within the framework of Section 115BBH. This could involve providing a specific formula for calculation, authorizing the CBDT to prescribe a methodology, or establishing a set of recognized valuation principles. By providing clarity and consistency in the valuation process, these measures would promote tax compliance, facilitate enforcement, and reduce the potential for disputes.

FAIR MARKET VALUE OF VDA

Determining the market value of cryptocurrencies presents several practical challenges. The inherent volatility of cryptocurrencies means their prices can fluctuate dramatically within short periods, making it difficult to pinpoint a precise market value at any given moment. This issue is further compounded by the fact that different cryptocurrency exchange platforms may offer varying prices for the same cryptocurrency simultaneously.

For example, if you were to check the price of Bitcoin on platforms like Wazirx, Coinbase, or Gemini at the same time, you might find slight discrepancies in their quoted prices. These price variations can arise due to factors such as differences in liquidity, trading volume, and the specific order book on each exchange.

Consequently, when determining the market value of a cryptocurrency for taxation or other purposes, it is crucial to consider these factors and potentially use a weighted average price from multiple exchanges to arrive at a more accurate valuation. Additionally, it may be necessary to consult with a qualified tax professional or financial advisor who specializes in cryptocurrency to ensure compliance with relevant regulations and optimize tax outcomes.

The Central Board of Direct Taxes (CBDT) should be granted the authority to establish rules for calculating the fair market value when virtual digital assets are transferred. However, if such guidance or rules are not available, the fair market value can be determined based on the price at which the asset is listed on an exchange platform on the date of the exchange or transfer.

In the case of an over-the-counter (OTC) deal or barter transaction, where a direct exchange of assets occurs without using an exchange platform, the taxpayer (assessee) might use the lowest value among all exchange platforms as the fair market value. This approach, although outlined in Rule 11UA for the valuation of shares or securities, can be applied to the valuation of virtual digital assets (VDAs) in the absence of specific guidance.

It is important to note that this is just one possible approach to determining the fair market value of VDAs in the absence of clear guidelines. Other methods may also be acceptable, and it is advisable to consult with a qualified tax professional for guidance on the best approach for specific situation

Additionally, it is worth noting that the regulatory landscape for VDAs is constantly evolving, and new guidance or rules may be issued by the CBDT or other relevant authorities in the future. It is therefore important to stay up-to-date on the latest developments in this area to ensure compliance with all applicable tax laws and regulations.

In case of conversion into stock-in-trade:

Thus, where VDA is converted into stock in trade in the year 2022-2023, but the stock is actually sold in the previous year 2023-2024, the capital gain shall be computed in the previous year 2022-2023 but liability to pay tax shall arise in the previous year 2023-2024.

In case of conversion from stock-in-trade:

Conversion of Virtual Digital Assets from Inventory to Capital Asset:

When Virtual Digital Assets (VDAs), which were initially held as inventory by a business, are converted into a capital asset, it triggers a taxable event. The tax liability arises from the difference between the fair market value of the VDAs at the time of conversion and their original cost of acquisition (if any). This difference is considered as business income and is taxable under Section 28(via) of the Income Tax Act.

Determining Fair Market Value:

The fair market value of the VDAs at the time of conversion is a crucial factor in calculating the taxable income. It is determined by the price that the VDAs would ordinarily fetch if they were sold in the open market on the date of conversion. This valuation ensures that the tax is levied on the actual market value of the VDAs at the time they transition from inventory to a capital asset.

METHOD FOR COMPUTATION OF COST OF ACQUISITION

When an individual engages in frequent buying and selling of Virtual Digital Assets (VDAs), determining the cost of acquisition for each VDA sold becomes crucial for accurate tax calculation. However, Section 115BBH of the Income Tax Act does not offer explicit guidance on how to establish this correlation.

To address this ambiguity, taxpayers can adopt either the First-In-First-Out (FIFO) method or the weighted average method to calculate the cost of acquisition for VDAs sold.

- The FIFO method assumes that the first VDA bought is also the first VDA sold. This approach aligns with the chronological order of transactions.

- The weighted average method calculates the average cost of all VDAs held, considering both the quantity and price of each acquisition. This method provides a blended cost basis for VDAs sold.

It is advisable to avoid the Last-In-First-Out (LIFO) method in the context of VDA transactions.

This is because the LIFO method assumes that the last VDA bought is the first VDA sold. Given the volatile nature of VDA markets, where purchase and sale prices can fluctuate significantly, the LIFO method may not accurately reflect the economic reality of the transactions and could lead to distorted tax outcomes.

The circular issued by the CBDT states that the First-In-First-Out (FIFO) method must be applied to ascertain the holding period for securities maintained in Demat form. However, due to the absence of explicit directions in Section 115BBH or a similar clarification from the CBDT concerning VDAs (Virtual Digital Assets), investors might consider adopting either the FIFO method or the weighted average method, based on which proves to be more advantageous in their specific situation.

It is crucial to remember that the aforementioned circular from the CBDT was issued specifically for securities. Given that VDAs might not be classified as securities, the applicability of the circular's guidance to VDAs is not definitively established. This distinction potentially creates ambiguity and a need for further clarification regarding the appropriate accounting method for determining the holding period of VDAs for taxation purposes.

The lack of clear guidance on this matter could lead to inconsistent practices among investors and potential disputes with tax authorities. Therefore, it is advisable for investors to seek professional advice and stay updated on any future clarifications or rulings from the CBDT regarding the taxation of VDAs, specifically concerning the determination of the holding period and the applicability of FIFO or weighted average methods.

In the FIFO method, the VDAs acquired last will be taken to be remaining with the assessee, while VDAs acquired first will be treated as sold. In the weighted average method, the cost of acquisition of the VDAs sold is the weighted average price of all his holdings at the time of sale.

COST OF ACQUISITION IN CASE OF MINING

When dealing with the taxation of cryptocurrencies, specifically the cost of acquisition for Virtual Digital Assets (VDAs) created through mining, it is essential to adhere to the Income-tax Act's guidelines. While the Act allows for expenditure incurred during the creation process to be considered as the cost of acquisition, it also specifies that certain costs may be disallowed under Section 55 and 115BBH.

However, the Act does not provide clear guidance on calculating the cost of acquisition for VDAs generated through mining. In the absence of specific rules, it is recommended that revenue expenditure directly related to mining operations be fully added to the cost of acquisition. Capital expenditure specific to mining, such as the cost of mining equipment, can be added to the cost of acquisition proportionally, based on the ratio of the asset mined during the year to the total mining capacity of the equipment.

It is crucial to note that any capital or revenue expenditure not directly related to the mining operation, but rather attributable to general operations, should be disallowed as part of the cost of acquisition. This area lacks clear guidelines and is open to interpretation, leading to potential disputes. Therefore, it is highly recommended that the Central Board of Direct Taxes (CBDT) issue a clarifying circular to provide explicit instructions on calculating the cost of acquisition for VDAs generated through mining. This would ensure consistency in tax treatment and reduce ambiguity for taxpayers and tax authorities alike.

Tax to be levied at 30%:

Section 115BBH(1) of the Income Tax Act outlines the specific tax treatment for income generated from the transfer of virtual digital assets. It stipulates that any profits realized from such transfers are subject to a **flat tax rate of 30%.**

This 30% tax rate is applicable **regardless of any other provisions** outlined in the Income Tax Act. This means that it overrides any other potential tax rates that might apply based on an individual's income bracket or the nature of other income sources.

In addition to the 30% base rate, the tax liability also includes any applicable **surcharge and cess**. These are additional charges levied on the base tax amount and can vary depending on the total income and other factors.

Key Points:

- **Flat Tax Rate:** The 30% rate applies uniformly to all gains from virtual digital asset transfers, irrespective of other income.

- **Overrides Other Provisions:** This section takes precedence over any conflicting tax rules in the Act.

- **Surcharge and Cess:** The total tax liability includes the 30% base rate plus any applicable surcharge and cess.

BENEFIT OF EXEMPTION LIMIT

In scenarios where an income is subject to taxation at a special rate as outlined in Chapter XII (Determination of tax in certain special cases) of the Income Tax Act, it's important to note that the general maximum exemption limit won't be applicable to such special income unless it is explicitly permitted within the relevant Section of the Act.

To illustrate, income that is calculated under Section 115BBH is subject to a flat tax rate of 30%. In this specific instance, the taxpayer is not entitled to the benefit of the basic exemption limit. This means that the entire income computed under Section 115BBH is subject to tax at the flat rate of 30%, regardless of whether it falls below the basic exemption limit.

REBATE UNDER SECTION 87A

Section 87A of the Income Tax Act provides a tax rebate to resident individuals whose total income for the previous year does not exceed Rs. 500,000. This rebate is capped at Rs. 60,000. In simpler terms, if the total tax payable, excluding cess, is equal to or less than Rs. 60,000, the taxpayer can claim the entire amount as a rebate.

This provision is generally available to all eligible taxpayers unless explicitly denied. For instance, income taxable under Section 112A is specifically excluded from the purview of the Section 87A rebate.

The Finance Act, 2025 has introduced a significant amendment that impacts the applicability of tax rebates. Specifically, the rebate provided under Section 87A of the Income Tax Act, which traditionally offered relief to taxpayers with income below a certain threshold, will no longer be available for income that is taxed at special rates.

This amendment essentially means that individuals or entities earning income that is subject to special tax rates, as prescribed by the Income Tax Act, will not be eligible to claim the Section 87A rebate. This change is likely to affect those with income from specific sources that are taxed differently from the regular income tax rates.

DEDUCTION UNDER CHAPTER VI-A

Deductions under Chapter VI-A and Section 115BBH:

Chapter VI-A of the Income Tax Act, 1961, outlines various deductions that taxpayers can claim to reduce their taxable income. These deductions encompass contributions to provident funds, life insurance premiums, and investments in specified schemes. However, it's crucial to note that **no deduction under Chapter VI-A is permissible from income computed under Section 115BBH**.

Section 115BBH pertains specifically to the taxation of income arising from the transfer of virtual digital assets (VDAs). This section stipulates a flat tax rate of 30% on such income, without the allowance of any deductions or exemptions except the cost of acquisition.

Implication:

The disallowance of Chapter VI-A deductions from income taxed under Section 115BBH implies that individuals or entities earning profits from VDA transfers cannot reduce their tax liability by claiming deductions for investments or insurance premiums.

This distinction underscores the government's intention to treat VDA income differently from other income sources for taxation purposes.

SECTION 115BBH(2)(A) PROHIBITS DEDUCTION

Section 115BBH(2)(a) prohibits deduction in respect of any:

- expenditure or allowance (other than cost of acquisition, if any);

- set off of any loss

TREATMENT OF LOSS

Let's break down Sub-section (2) of Section 115BBH, which begins with a non obstante clause and contains two crucial clauses:

Clause (a): Prohibition of Loss Set-Off:

This clause explicitly states that when calculating the income as defined in Section 115BBH(1)(a), the assessee is not allowed to set off any losses against it. This means that any losses incurred cannot be used to reduce the taxable income from the transfer of virtual digital assets (VDAs).

Clause (b): No Set-Off and No Carry Forward of Losses:

This clause further reinforces the restriction on loss utilization. It specifies that any loss resulting from the transfer of VDA, as computed under Section 115BBH(1)(a), cannot be set off against any other income computed under any other provision of the Income Tax Act. Moreover, it prohibits the carry forward of such losses to subsequent assessment years. This implies that losses from VDA transactions are isolated and cannot be used to offset gains in other income streams or in future years.

Non Obstante Clause:

The presence of the non obstante clause at the beginning of Sub-section (2) signifies that the provisions of this sub-section override any other contradictory provisions in the Income Tax Act. It emphasizes the intention of the legislature to treat income from the transfer of VDAs distinctly and prevent any form of loss set-off or carry forward in relation to such income.

Overall Impact:

The combined effect of these clauses is to create a tax regime for VDA transactions where losses are ring-fenced and cannot be used to reduce the overall tax liability. This approach ensures that income from VDA transfers is taxed at the specified rate without any deductions for losses.

Key Points to Remember:

- Losses from VDA transfers cannot be set off against any other income.
- Losses from VDA transfers cannot be carried forward to future years.
- The provisions of Sub-section (2) override any conflicting provisions in the Income Tax Act.

Both the clauses attempt to ring-fence the losses arising from VDA. It neither allows any loss to set-off against income from VDA nor allows loss from VDA to set-off against income computed under any provision of the Income-tax Act, 1961.

Let's delve deeper into the implications of the tax provision as mentioned in the clause.

Breakdown of the Clause:

The clause states that losses incurred from the transfer of Virtual Digital Assets (VDAs) cannot be adjusted against any other income, even income from the transfer of another VDA. This is due to the specific wording "any provision of this Act," which encompasses all sections, including Section 115BBH that deals with income from VDA transfers.

Implications for Investors:

This essentially means that if an investor experiences a loss on the sale of a VDA, they cannot offset that loss against gains from the sale of another VDA. This is a significant departure from the treatment of other capital assets where losses can often be used to offset gains for tax purposes. Each VDA transaction is treated in isolation for tax purposes.

Dead Loss Scenario:

The term "dead loss" aptly describes the situation. A loss on a VDA transaction is essentially unrecoverable and cannot be used to reduce the overall tax burden. This can have a substantial impact on the profitability of VDA investments, as investors need to factor in the potential for unrecoverable losses.

Impact on Investment Strategy:

This tax treatment may necessitate a more cautious approach to VDA investments. Investors need to be even more diligent in their research and analysis, as the potential for unrecoverable losses increases the risk associated with VDA investments. Diversification across different VDA categories may also be less effective as a risk management strategy, as losses in one category cannot be offset against gains in another.

Need for Clarity:

The stringent tax treatment of VDA losses highlights the need for greater clarity and guidance in the tax regulations surrounding VDAs. As the VDA market continues to evolve, it is crucial that tax policies keep pace and provide a clear and predictable framework for investors.

Losses incurred on or before assessment year 2022-23–Section 115BBH(2) prohibits carrying forward and setting-off of losses from VDAs with effect from the assessment year 2023-24. Would such provision impact the losses incurred on or before the assessment year 2022-23? In other words, can such losses be carried forward and set-off with income taxable under the relevant head (except income from transfer of VDA) in the assessment year 2023-24 and onwards.

A similar issue was dealt with by the Supreme Court in the case of CIT v. Shah Sadiq & Sons [1987] 1987 AIR 1217 (SC). The apex court held that under the 1922 Act, the assessee was entitled to carry forward the losses of the speculation business and set off such losses against profits made from that business in future years. The right of carrying forward and set off accrued to the assessee under the 1922 Act. A right that had accrued and had become vested continued to be capable of being enforced notwithstanding the repeal of the statute under which that right accrued unless the repealing statute took away such right expressly. The 'savings' provision in the repealing statute is not exhaustive of the rights which are saved or which survive the repeal of the statute under which such rights had accrued. In other words, whatever rights are expressly saved by the 'savings' provision stand saved. But, that does not mean that rights that are not saved by the 'savings' provision are extinguished or stand ipso facto terminated by the mere fact that a new statute repealing the old statute is enacted. Rights that have accrued are saved unless they are taken away expressly. In the circumstances, the assessee was entitled to the set off in the assessment year 1963-64.

Thus, the assessee should have an absolute right to carry forward and set-off the losses incurred on or before the assessment year 2022-23. However, such losses shall not be allowed to set-off against income taxable under Section 115BBH. Such rights can be exercised within the four corners of the provisions specified in Section 72, 73, 74 read with Section 80.

TRANSFER OF VIRTUAL DIGITAL ASSET WITHOUT OR INADEQUATE CONSIDERATION

The transfer of a Virtual Digital Asset (VDA) can occur in various scenarios:

- **For Consideration:** This involves the exchange of a VDA for fiat currency, another virtual currency or digital asset, or for goods and services. Such transfers are subject to taxation under Section 115BBH.

- **Without Consideration:** This encompasses scenarios where a VDA is transferred without a reciprocal exchange of value, such as gifts or inheritance.

  - **Transferor:** The transfer of a VDA without consideration is tax-neutral for the transferor.

  - **Recipient:** The recipient of the VDA is liable to pay tax under Section 56(2)(x) or Section 28(iv).

Therefore, the tax implications of a VDA transfer hinge on whether the transfer is made for consideration or without consideration, with different tax provisions applicable in each scenario.

UPDATES IN THE FINANCE ACT, 2022

New entry inserted by the Finance Act, 2022 – With effect from the assessment year 2023-24, the Finance Act, 2022 inserted 'virtual digital assets' in the meaning of property [Explanation (d) to section 56(2) (vii)]. Thus, after the amendment, property shall mean:

(a) Shares and securities;

(b) Jewellery;

(c) Archaeological collections;

(d) Drawings;

(e) Paintings;

(f) Sculptures;

(g) Any work of art;

(h) Bullion; and

(i) Virtual Digital Asset

Exemption from taxability:

Deemed Income and Virtual Digital Assets (VDAs): Exceptions:

Under Section 115BBH of the Income Tax Act, and other relevant provisions, income from Virtual Digital

Assets (VDAs) is generally subject to taxation. However, certain situations are exempt from this deemed income rule, specifically when VDAs are received under circumstances mentioned in the Proviso to Section 56(2)(x). These exceptions include:

- **VDAs received on the occasion of marriage:** Any VDAs received by an individual as a gift on the occasion of their marriage are exempt from being considered as deemed income. This aligns with the general exemption for marriage gifts under tax laws.

- **VDAs received under a will or by way of inheritance:** VDAs acquired through inheritance or as a bequest under a will are not considered deemed income. This is consistent with the tax treatment of inherited assets in general.

- **VDAs received in contemplation of death:** If VDAs are gifted in contemplation of the payer's or donor's death, they are not treated as deemed income. This exception recognizes the unique circumstances surrounding gifts made in anticipation of death.

- **VDAs received from any specified relative:** VDAs received from specified relatives as gifts are exempt from deemed income. The term "specified relative" is defined within the Income Tax Act and typically includes close family members.

Key Point: These exceptions ensure that legitimate transfers of VDAs in personal and family contexts are not subject to unnecessary taxation. It is crucial to remember that these exemptions apply only to the specific circumstances mentioned and do not extend to other situations where VDAs are received.

TAXABILITY UNDER SECTION 28(IV) – BUSINESS INCOME

If such tokens are given without any consideration (cash or in-kind), it will be taxable under Section 56(2)(x). Where in consideration of such tokens, the influencer has to do some marketing, by way of a Tweet, YouTube video, Instagram Reel, any other social media post, or writing a blog, the market value of such token shall be taxable under Section 28(iv) in the hands of the recipient, provided the recipient is carrying on a business. In such a situation, the provider shall ensure that the tax has been deducted in respect of such benefits or perquisites under Section 194R

TAXABILITY UNDER SECTION 56(2)(X) – OTHER SOURCE INCOME

In scenarios where income is subject to taxation under Section 56(2)(x), the market value of the property in question is determined in accordance with Rule 11UA. However, a discrepancy arises when income is taxable under Section 28(iv). In these instances, the Central Board of Direct Taxes (CBDT) lacks the authority to prescribe any rule for determining the market value of a benefit or perquisite that arises from a business or profession.

This lack of empowerment creates a gap in the tax framework, as there is no clear mechanism to establish the fair market value for the purposes of Section 28(iv). To rectify this inconsistency and ensure a comprehensive and equitable tax system, it is imperative that the necessary amendments be made. These amendments should specifically empower the CBDT to formulate and implement rules for the computation of fair market value within the context of Section 28(iv).

By addressing this legislative gap and granting the CBDT the authority to establish clear guidelines for valuation under Section 28(iv), the tax system can be strengthened and made more consistent. This would provide greater clarity for taxpayers and tax authorities alike, reducing ambiguity and potential disputes regarding the valuation of benefits and perquisites arising from business or professional activities.

TAX RATES IF TAXED UNDER SECTION 28(IV) OR 56(2)(X)

Let's delve deeper into the tax implications highlighted in the original text.

Taxation of Benefits under Section 56(2)(x) and Section 28(iv):

When a benefit arises under Section 56(2)(x) or Section 28(iv), its value is taxed at the applicable rate for the assessee. This essentially means that the tax rate will depend on the total income and applicable tax bracket of the individual or entity receiving the benefit.

Exclusion from 30% Tax under Section 115BBH:

It's crucial to note that such income is not taxed at the flat rate of 30% under Section 115BBH. This is because the income doesn't originate from the transfer of a virtual digital asset. Section 115BBH specifically deals with income arising from the transfer of virtual digital assets and taxes it at a special rate.

Taxation of Subsequent Transfers:

However, the scenario changes when the recipient of the benefit decides to transfer the virtual digital assets further. Any gains resulting from this subsequent transfer will fall under the purview of Section 115BBH. Consequently, these gains will be taxed at the 30% rate stipulated in that section.

Key Points to Remember:

- Benefits under Section 56(2)(x) and Section 28(iv) are taxed at the assessee's applicable rate.

- These benefits are not taxed at 30% under Section 115BBH as they don't arise from the transfer of virtual digital assets.

- Gains from the subsequent transfer of such assets by the recipient are taxable under Section 115BBH at 30%.

Overall, the taxation of benefits and gains related to virtual digital assets is a nuanced area with specific provisions for different scenarios. It is important to understand these distinctions to ensure compliance with tax regulations and avoid potential penalties.

COST OF ACQUISITION OF VDAS RECEIVED AS GIFT

Where the VDA is received as gift, the cost of acquisition thereof shall depend whether it is capital asset or trading asset in the hands of recipient.

Where the VDA is received as capital asset, the cost for which the previous owner acquired it shall be treated as cost of acquisition. However, if the value of the VDA is charged to tax in the hands of recipient under section 56(2)(x) at the time of receipt thereof, then such value shall be considered as cost of acquisition [section 49].

Where the gift of VDA is received as stock-in-trade, the cost of such VDA in the hands of the recipient shall be determined as per Section 145A read with ICDS-II (Valuation of Inventories).

Section 145A provides that the valuation of inventory shall be made at lower of actual cost or net realisable value computed in accordance with the ICDS-II. Para 4 of ICDS-II provides that cost of inventories shall comprise of all costs of purchase, other costs incurred in bringing the inventories to their present location and condition. Para 5 provides that the costs of purchase shall consist of purchase price including duties and taxes, freight inwards and other expenditure directly attributable to the acquisition. As the purchase price is nil, the value of VDA, being inventory, shall also be nil. However, if the donee has paid any legal charges, stamp duty or tax in respect of the gift, it should be included in the value of such inventory.

DEDUCTION OF TAX AT SOURCE UNDER SECTION 194S

Section 194S of the Income Tax Act has been introduced to govern the taxation of virtual digital assets (VDAs). This section mandates the **deduction of tax at source (TDS)** on payments made for the transfer of VDAs.

Key Points:

- **Applicability:** This provision came into effect on **July 1, 2022**.

- **TDS on VDA Transfers:** Any person responsible for paying consideration for the transfer of a VDA is required to deduct TDS.

- **Scope:** The term "virtual digital asset" encompasses a wide range of digital assets, including cryptocurrencies and non-fungible tokens (NFTs).

- **Tax Rate and Threshold:** The tax rate and threshold limit for TDS on VDA transfers are specified by the Income Tax Department and may vary depending on the type of VDA and the nature of the transaction.

- **Compliance:** It is crucial for both payers and payees to adhere to the TDS provisions under Section 194S to avoid penalties and legal complications.

Purpose:

- The introduction of Section 194S aims to **bring more transparency and accountability** to the VDA market.

- By mandating TDS on VDA transfers, the government intends to **track transactions** and **ensure that taxes are paid** on gains arising from such transfers.

Implications:

- Section 194S has **significant implications for investors, traders, and businesses** operating in the VDA space.

- It is essential for stakeholders to **understand their tax obligations** and **comply with the TDS provisions** to avoid any adverse consequences.

- The introduction of this provision also **reflects the growing recognition** of VDAs as a legitimate asset class by the government.

Who is Deductor:

Any person (resident or non-resident) responsible for paying any sum by way of consideration for the transfer of a virtual digital asset is required to deduct tax at source.

Applicability of TDS when consideration in kind:

In scenarios involving the exchange of Virtual Digital Assets (VDAs), it's important to recognize that the transfer of these assets occurs on both sides of the transaction. This means that both the payer and the payee are involved in the transfer of VDAs. Due to this dual transfer, both parties may be liable to deduct tax at source (TDS) as per Section 194S of the Income Tax Act.

This essentially implies that when two parties exchange VDAs, each party is considered to have transferred a VDA to the other. As a result, both parties may have tax withholding obligations under the relevant tax laws. It is crucial for both parties to be aware of these potential tax implications and to ensure compliance with TDS regulations to avoid any penalties or legal consequences.

Receipt of VDA as Consideration of Services:

Further, where a person receives the VDAs as consideration for his services, he shall be responsible for deducting tax at source. For example, an architect will be a deductor if he gets his fees for technical services in the form of VDAs. The tax shall be deducted under this provision because he is giving the consideration in the form of architecture services to the person transferring the VDA to him.

Deductee:

Tax is required to be deducted under this provision if the consideration is paid or payable to any resident person. If the recipient of the consideration is any non-resident, the tax may be deductible under Section 195.

In the context of tax regulations, the deduction of tax at source is a crucial mechanism to ensure compliance and timely collection of revenue. The given provision emphasizes that the obligation to deduct tax arises when the consideration (payment) is made or is due to a resident person. This means that if the recipient of the payment is a resident of the country, the payer is legally required to deduct the applicable tax amount from the payment and remit it to the government.

However, the situation differs when the recipient of the consideration is a non-resident. In such cases, the deductibility of tax is governed by Section 195 of the Income Tax Act. This section deals with the tax deduction on payments made to non-residents and provides a framework for determining whether tax should be deducted, the applicable tax rate, and the procedures for deduction and remittance.

It is important to note that the wording "tax may be deductible" under Section 195 implies that the deduction of tax in the case of non-residents is not always mandatory. It depends on various factors such as the nature of the payment, the tax residency status of the non-resident, the existence of a Double Taxation Avoidance Agreement (DTAA), and the specific provisions of the DTAA, if applicable.

Therefore, while tax deduction at source is obligatory for payments to residents, it is contingent and subject to specific conditions for payments to non-residents. The payer must carefully assess the tax residency status of the recipient and consult the provisions of Section 195 and any relevant DTAA to determine the tax implications and their obligation to deduct tax.

RATE OF TDS

In accordance with the current tax regulations, a 1% tax rate is mandated to be deducted from the consideration amount. This specified rate is inclusive of all applicable charges and will not be subject to any further increment on account of Surcharge or Health & Education Cess.

It is obligatory for the deductee to furnish their Permanent Account Number (PAN) to the deductor. Failure to comply with this requirement will result in the application of a higher tax deduction rate. As per the provisions under Section 206AA, the tax deduction rate, in the absence of a furnished PAN, will be 20% of the consideration amount.

Time of deduction:

In the realm of cryptocurrency taxation, the deduction of tax occurs at the earliest of two points: when payment is made through any method, or when the sum is credited to the resident's account. This implies that the tax liability arises and must be addressed at the moment of transaction or when the proceeds are reflected in the account, whichever happens first.

Furthermore, the tax treatment for intra-day trading of cryptocurrencies necessitates tax deduction at each instance a transaction is squared-off. Intraday trading refers to the practice of buying and selling cryptocurrencies within the same trading day, with the intention of profiting from short-term price fluctuations. In such scenarios, every time a position is closed or squared-off, meaning the buy transaction is matched with a corresponding sell transaction, the tax liability is triggered, and the tax must be deducted accordingly.

This approach ensures that tax is collected on each profitable trade, preventing any potential for tax evasion through the rapid buying and selling of cryptocurrencies within a single day. It also aligns with the principle of taxing income as it is earned, as each squared-off transaction represents a realized profit or loss that is subject to taxation.

AMOUNT ON WHICH TAX IS TO BE DEDUCTED

Tax is required to be deducted from the gross amount of consideration paid to the resident person for the transfer of virtual digital assets.

However, in the following cases, before releasing the consideration, the person responsible shall ensure that tax required to be deducted has been paid in respect of such consideration for the transfer of virtual digital asset:

- Where consideration is wholly in kind;

- Where a transaction is in exchange for another virtual digital asset, and there is no part in cash; or

- Where consideration is partly in cash and partly in kind, but the part in cash is not sufficient to meet the liability of deduction of tax in respect of whole of such transfer.

Consideration is below Rs. 10,000 – No tax shall be deducted under this provision if the consideration is payable by any person (other than a specified person) and its aggregate value does not exceed Rs. 10,000 during the financial year [Section 194S(3)(b)].

Consideration is below Rs. 50,000 – No tax shall be deducted under this provision if the consideration is payable by the following specified persons and its aggregate value does not exceed Rs. 50,000 during the financial year:

- An individual or a HUF, whose total sales, gross receipts or turnover does not exceed Rs. 1 crore in case of business or Rs. 50 lakh in case of a profession, during the financial year immediately preceding the financial year in which such virtual digital asset is transferred;

- An individual or a HUF who does not have any income under the head profits and gains of business or profession [Section 194S(3)(a) read with Explanation to section 194S].

OVERRIDING EFFECT OF TDS PROVISION

Multiple TDS provisions applicable to payer – Where a transaction is subject to TDS under Section 194-O and Section 194S, tax shall be deducted under Section 194S. Similarly, where a transaction is covered under Section 194S, Section 194-O and Section 206C(1H), the tax should be deducted under Section 194S, because where a transaction is covered under both Section 194-O and Section 206C(1H), the tax is deducted under Section 194-O by virtue of CBDT's Circular No. 20/2021 dated 25th November 2021. Since Section 194S is preferred over Section 194-O due to sub-section (4) of Section 194S; eventually, tax deduction should be made under Section 194S.

TDS provisions applicable to both payer and payee:

Where payer deducts tax under Section 194S, it shall not absolve the payee from deduction of tax under relevant provisions. For example, if an architect receives bitcoin from his client as consideration for services, then the architect shall be liable to deduct tax under section 194S as he is giving the consideration in the form of architecture services to the client transferring the VDA and, on the other side, the client may also be liable to deduct tax under section 194J as he is making payment in form of VDA for services provided by the architect.

TAN IS NOT MANDATORY

Specified person as defined above does not require to apply or obtain a Tax Deduction or Collection Account Number (TAN) for deducting tax under this provision [Section 194S(2)]. However, such a deductor shall be required to quote his PAN in challan and TDS statement as required by sub-section (5) and sub-section (5B) of section 139A.

NO TDS ON GIFT OR LENDING OF VDAs

Section 194S applies when the consideration is paid in respect of transfer of VDAs. As gift or lending of VDA does not fall in definition of transfer, no tax shall be deducted in such cases.

The tax deducted is required to be reported to the government in Form 26QE. Form 26QE is a prescribed challan-cum-statement of TDS.

Example:

Sunil buys 1 ETH for ₹1,00,000 on July 1, 2022, and pays ₹100 as brokerage.

He sells 1 ETH for ₹2,00,000 and pays ₹200 as brokerage.

Let us find out his Profit and Tax amount.

As we know, Profit = (Sale Price – Buy Price)* Quantity sold

So, Sunil's profit = ₹2,00,000–₹1,00,000 * 1 (ETH)

Profit = ₹1,00,000

TDS at 1% deducted by the exchange on Sale of 1 ETH for ₹2,00,000 = ₹2,000

Tax at the time of return filing:

Profit = ₹1,00,000

Tax at 30% on Profit = ₹30,000

Less: TDS = ₹2,000

Balance Tax to be paid = ₹28,000

AIRDROPS

Airdrops will be taxed as Income from other Sources only if they have value – as on the date of receipt and are traded on exchanges.

Example 1:

Sunil received 10,000 ABC tokens as Airdrop on April 01, 2022.

There is no trading of ABC tokens either on exchanges or DEXs.

In this case, Sunil will not have any income from airdrops.

Example 2:

Anil received 10,000 ABC tokens as Airdrop on April 01, 2022. There is a trading of ABC tokens on exchanges. ABC token is quoting a price of ₹10 on April 01, 2022.

In this case, Anil will have an Income from airdrops of ₹1,00,000/- at the time of receipt of airdrops.

In example 2, if subsequent sale:

Sunil received 10,000 ABC tokens as Airdrop on April 01, 2022. There is no trading of ABC tokens either on exchanges or DEXs.

If Anil sold the tokens on June 03, 2022, when the price was ₹20 per ABC token then the taxable gains will be 10,000 ABC tokens * (₹20–₹10) = ₹1,00,000 taxed at 30% this amount (₹1,00,000/-) will be considered as a cost for computing gains on the subsequent sale of the tokens.

MINTING TOKENS

Minting involves generating new tokens on the blockchain. Usually, apart from gas fees and infrastructure costs no other costs are incurred. Hence, these transactions may not be a taxable event.

Example:

Varun minted his own token VRN on Blockchain and incurred gas fees of ₹10 to mint the tokens.

In this case, there is no taxable Income.

REFERRAL REWARDS

Referral rewards are rewards received by referring users to projects. This will be taxed as Income from other sources (IFOS) or as business income.

Example:

Sunil received 10 USDT as Referral rewards on April 30, 2022. The value of 1 USDT as on April 30 is ₹80.

In this case, Sunil will have Income from Referral rewards of ₹800 (10 USDT * ₹80). It is taxable as income from other sources or as business income.

CENTRAL BOARD OF DIRECT TAXES (CBDT) CIRCULAR NO. 13 OF 2022

Question 1. Who is required to deduct tax when the transfer of VDA is taking place on or through an Exchange and payment is made by the purchaser to the Exchange (directly or through broker) and then from the Exchange it goes to seller directly or through the broker?

Answer: According to section 194S of the Act, any person who is responsible for paying to any resident any sum by way of consideration for transfer of VDA is required to deduct tax. Thus, in a peer to peer (i.e. direct buyer to seller) transaction, the buyer (i.e person paying the consideration) is required to deduct tax under section 194S of the Act.

However, if the transaction is taking place on or through an Exchange there is a possibility of tax deduction requirement under section 194S of the Act at multiple stages. Hence, in order to remove difficulties for transactions taking place on or through an Exchange, the following clarifications are issued:-

(i) In a case where the transfer of VDA takes place on or through an Exchange and the VDA being transferred is owned by a person other than the

Exchange: In this case buyer would be crediting or making payment to the Exchange (directly or through a broker). The Exchange then would be required to credit or make payment to the owner of VDA being transferred, either directly or through a broker. Since there are multiple players, to remove difficulty it is clarified that:

1. Tax may be deducted under section 194S of the Act only by the Exchange which is crediting or making payment to the seller (owner of the VDA being transferred). In a case where broker owns the VDA, it is the broker who is the seller. Hence, the amount of consideration being credited or paid to the broker by the Exchange is also subject to tax deduction under section 194S of the Act.

2. In a case where the credit/payment between Exchange and the seller is through a broker (and the broker is not seller), the responsibility to deduct tax under section 194S of the Act shall be on both the Exchange and the broker. However, if there is a written agreement between the Exchange and the broker that broker shall be deducting tax on such credit/payment, then broker alone may deduct the tax under section 194S of the Act. The Exchange would be required to furnish a quarterly statement (in Form no

26QF) for all such transactions of the quarter on or before the due date prescribed in the Income-tax Rules, 1962. The due dates are as:

Quarter	Due date
Q1	31 July
Q2	31 October
Q3	31 January
Q4	31 May

(ii) In a case where the transfer of VDA takes place on or through an Exchange and the VDA being transferred is owned by such Exchange: In this case there are no multiple players. The buyer is required to deduct tax under section 194S of the Act. However, there may be a practical issue as the buyer may not know whether the VDA being transferred is owned by the Exchange or not. Hence, there may be genuine doubt in the mind of buyer with regard to its responsibility to deduct tax under section 194S of the Act. This difficulty would also be there if the buyer is buying VDA from an Exchange through a broker.

To remove this difficulty, it is clarified that while the primary responsibility to deduct tax under section 194S of the Act, in this case, remains with the buyer or his broker, as an alternative the Exchange may enter into a written agreement with the buyer or his broker that in regard to all such transactions the Exchange would be paying the tax on or before the due date for that quarter. The Exchange would be required to furnish a quarterly statement (in Form No. 26QF) for all such transactions of the quarter on or before the due date prescribed in the Income-tax Rules, 1962. The Exchange would also be required to furnish its income tax return and all these transactions must be included in such return. If these conditions are complied with, the buyer or his broker would not be held as assessee in default under section 201 of the Act for these transactions.

For the purpose of this circular,-

(i) The term "Exchange" means any person that operates an application or platform for transferring of VDAs, which matches buy and sell trades and executes the same on its application or platform.

(ii) The term "Broker" means any person that operates an application or platform for transferring of VDAs and holds brokerage account/accounts with an Exchange for execution of such trades.

Question 2: Question no 1 was with respect to transactions where the consideration for transfer of VDA is not in kind. How will this operate in a situation where it is in kind or in exchange of another VDA?

Answer: According to proviso to sub-section (1) of section 194S of the Act, there could be situations where the consideration is in kind or in exchange of another VDA or partly in kind and cash is not sufficient to meet the TDS liability. In these situations, the person responsible for paying such consideration is required to ensure that tax required to be deducted has been paid in respect of such consideration, before releasing the consideration.

In the above situation, the buyer will release the consideration in kind after seller provides proof of payment of such tax (e.g. Challan details etc.). In a situation where VDA "A" is being exchanged with another VDA "B", both the persons are buyer as well as seller. One is buyer for "A" and seller for "B" and another is buyer for "B" and seller for "A". Thus both need to pay tax with respect to transfer of VDA and show the evidence to other so that VDAs can then be exchanged. This would then be required to be reported in TDS statement along with challan number. This year Form No. 26Q has included provisions for reporting such transactions. For specified persons, Form No. 26QE has been introduced.

However, if the transaction is through an Exchange there is practical issue in implementing this provision. In order to address this practical issue and to remove difficulty, it is clarified that in such a situation, as an alternative, tax may be deducted by the Exchange. Such an alternative mechanism can be exercised by the Exchange based on written contractual agreement with the buyers/sellers.

If such an alternative mechanism is exercised,

i.   the Exchange would be required to deduct tax for both legs of the transactions and pay to the Government. In the Form 26Q it will, for the reasons explained before, need to report it as tax deducted on both legs of the transaction.

ii.   the buyer and seller would not be independently required to follow the procedure prescribed in proviso to sub-section (1) of section 194S of the Act.

When the Exchange opts for deduction of tax under section 194S of the Act on such transactions, there is also a possibility that the tax amount deducted is also in kind and needs to be converted into cash before it can be deposited with the Government. In this regard, the following mechanism shall be adopted by the Exchange

1.   At the time of transaction, the Exchange will deduct TDS in the pair being traded. For example, in case of trade for Monero to Deso, 1% of Monero and 1% Deso will be deducted

as tax under section 194S of the Act by the Exchange and balance shall be transferred to the customer. The trail of transactions evidencing deduction of 1% of consideration for every VDA to VDA trade shall be maintained by the Exchange.

2. The Exchanges shall immediately execute a market order for converting this tax deducted in kind (1% Monero/ 1% Deso in the above example) to one of the primary VDAs (BT, ETH, USDT, USDC) which can be easily converted into INR. This step will ensure that the tax deducted under section 194S of the Act in the form of non-primary VDAs like Deso/Monero is converted to an equivalent of primary VDAs which have a ready INR market. Time stamps of timing of orders to be maintained to ensure such conversion of VDAs withheld to be done on immediate basis by the Exchange. If the taxes are withheld in primary VDAs, this step would be ignored.

3. All the tax deducted under section 194S of the Act in the form of primary VDAs {or converted into primary VDA under step (ii)} will be accumulated for the day. Time limit will be from 00:00 hours to 23:59 hours. VDA accumulation

by the Exchange shall be verifiable from the trail of orders for VDA to VDA trades executed during the day.

4. The accumulated balance of primary VDAs at 00.00 hours will be converted into INR based on the market rate existing at that time. In order to bring in consistency and to avoid discretion, the Exchanges are required to place market order at 00:00 hours for the tax withheld {or converted under step (ii)} in form of primary VDAs for conversion into INR. These sell market orders shall be executed based on the open buy orders in the market. Price and quantity data for every matched trade shall be maintained by the Exchange and shall be available for verification. It shall be verifiable from the system coding that the conversion into INR happened at the first available buy order based on the prevailing buy order book of the respective Exchange at the time of conversion. As a practice, the respective Exchange liquidating the VDA shall be prohibited to be a buyer for these VDAs.

5. Customer will be issued a contract note over email which will include the amount of tax withheld in kind under section 194S and the amount of INR realized from such tax withheld.

6. The tax withheld in kind under section 194S of the Act and converted into INR by following the above procedure shall be deposited in the Government Account as per the time line (7th day of the month following the month in which the tax was deducted) and process given in the Income-tax Rules 1962.

It is clarified that there would not be any further TDS for converting the tax withheld in kind in the form of VDA into INR or from one VDA to another VDA and then into INR.

Question 3: Whether the provision of section 194Q of the Act is also applicable on transfer of VDA?

Answer: Without going into the merit whether VDA is goods or not, it is clarified that once tax is deducted under section 194S of the Act, tax would not be required to be deducted under section 194Q of the Act.

Question 4: Whether the consideration for transfer of VDA shall be on Gross basis after including GST/commission or it shall be on "net basis" after exclusion of these items.

Answer: In order to remove difficulty, it is clarified that the tax required to be withheld under section 194S of the Act shall be on the "net" consideration after excluding GST/charges levied by the deductor for rendering service

Question 5: In transactions where payment is being carried out through payment gateways, there may be tax deduction twice. To illustrate that a person 'XYZ' is required to make payment to the seller for transfer of VDA. He makes payment of one lakh rupees through digital platform of "ABC". On these facts liability to deduct tax under section 194S of the Act may fall on both "XYZ" and "ABC. Is tax required to be deducted by both?

Answer: In order to remove this difficulty, it is provided that in the above example, the payment gateway will not be required to deduct tax under section 194S of the Act on a transaction, if the tax has been deducted by the person ('XYZ') required to make deduction under section 194S of the Act. Hence, in the above example, if "XYZ" has deducted tax under section 194S of the Act on one lakh rupees, "ABC" will not be required to deduct tax under section 194S of the Act on the same transaction. To facilitate proper implementation,"ABC" may take an undertaking from "XYZ" regarding deduction of tax.

Question 6: Section 194S shall come into effect from the 1st July 2022. The liability to deduct tax under section 194S of the Act applies only when the value or aggregate value of the consideration for transfer of VDA exceeds fifty thousand rupees during the financial year in case of consideration being paid by specified person and ten thousand rupees in other cases. It is not clear how this limit of fifty thousand (or ten thousand) is to be computed?

Answer: It is clarified that,-

- Since the threshold of fifty thousand rupees (or ten thousand rupees) is with respect to the financial year, calculation of consideration for transfer of VDA triggering deduction under section 194S of the Act shall be counted from 1st April, 2022. Hence, if the value or aggregate value of the consideration for transfer of VDA payable by a person exceeds fifty thousand rupees (or ten thousand rupees) during the financial year 2022-23 (including the period up to 30th June 2022), the provision of section 194S of the Act shall apply on any sum, representing consideration for transfer of VDA, credited or paid on or after 1st July 2022.

- Since the provision of section 194S of the Act applies at the time of credit or payment (whichever is earlier) of any sum, representing consideration for transfer of VDA, such sum which has been credited or paid before 1st July 2022 would not be subjected to tax deduction under section 194S of the Act.

CENTRAL BOARD OF DIRECT TAXES (CBDT) CIRCULAR NO. 14 OF 2022

1) Liability to deduct tax at source under section 194S of the Act when the consideration is other than in kind.

According to section 194S of the Act, any person who is responsible for paying to any resident any sum by way of consideration for transfer of VDA is required to deduct tax. Thus,in a peer to peer (i.e. buyer to seller without going through an Exchange) transaction, the buyer (i.e person paying the consideration) is required to deduct tax under section 194S of the Act. The tax so deducted is required to be deposited with Government in accordance with the time and procedure prescribed in the Act read with the relevant provisions of the Income-tax Rules, 1962.

After deduction, the deductor is required to furnish a quarterly statement (in Form No.26Q) for all such transactions of the quarter on or before the due date prescribed in the Income-taxRules, 1962. For specified person Form 26QE has been introduced.

It may be clarified that the TDS shall be on consideration for transfer of VDA less GST.

2) Liability to deduct tax at source under section 194S of the Act when the consideration is in kind or in exchange of VDA

According to the proviso to sub-section (1) of section 194S of the Act, there could be a situation where the consideration is in kind or in exchange of another VDA or partly in kind and cash is not sufficient to meet the TDS liability. In this situation, the person responsible for paying such consideration is required to ensure that tax required to be deducted has been paid in respect of such consideration, before releasing the consideration.

Thus, the buyer will release the consideration in kind after seller provides proof of payment of such tax (e.g. challan details etc.). In a situation where VDA "A" is being exchanged with another VDA "B", both the persons are buyer as well as seller. One is buyer for "A" and seller for "B" and another is buyer for "B" and seller for "A". Thus both need to pay tax with respect to transfer of VDA and show the evidence to other so that VDAs can then be exchanged. This would then be required to be reported in TDS statement along with challan number by both of them. This year Form 26Q has included provisions for reporting such transactions. For specified persons, Form 26QE has been introduced.

3) Interplay between provision of section 194S and section 194Q

Without going into the merit whether VDA is goods or not, it is clarified that once tax is deducted under section 194S of the Act, tax would not be required to be deducted under section 194Q of the Act.

CHANGES AS PROPOSED IN FINANCE BILL 2025

Enlargement of scope of coverage of Virtual Digital Assets:

It is also proposed to amend clause (47A) of section 2 to insert sub-clause (d) which states that the definition of virtual digital asset also includes any crypto-asset being a digital representation of value that relies on a cryptographically secured distributed ledger or a similar technology to validate and secure transactions, whether or not already included in the definition of virtual digital asset or not.

Amendments proposed in provisions of Block assessment for search and requisition cases:

Vide Finance (No. 2) Act, 2024, the concept of block assessment was introduced by amending provisions of Chapter XIV-B (sections 158B to 158BI of the Act) to be made applicable where a search under section 132 of the Act is initiated or requisition under section 132A of the Act is made, on or after 01st September, 2024.

Section 158B of the Act defines "undisclosed income" for the purposes of Chapter XIV-B. It is proposed to add the term "virtual digital asset" to the said definition.

In Section 158B, addition of virtual digital assets along with money, bullion, jewellery enlarges the scope of block assessment in search cases by specifically inserting virtual digital assets.

As per The Finance Bill, 2025 A new Section 285BAA proposed to be inserted in the Act, being the Obligation to furnish information of crypto-asset, wherein –

(I) Sub-section (1) of section 285BAA of the Act states any person, being a reporting entity, as may be prescribed, in respect of crypto asset, shall furnish information in respect of a transaction in such crypto asset in a statement, for such period, within such time, in such form and manner and to such income-tax authority, as may be prescribed;

(II) Sub-section (2) of said section states that where prescribed income-tax authority considers that the statement furnished is defective, he may intimate the defect to the person who has furnished such statement and give him an opportunity of rectifying the defect within a period of thirty days from the date of such intimation or such further period as may be allowed, and if the defect is not rectified within the aforesaid period allowed, the provisions of this Act shall apply as if such person had furnished inaccurate information in the statement;

(III) Sub-section (3) of said section states that where a person who is required to furnish a statement has not furnished the same within the specified time, the prescribed income-tax authority may serve upon such person a notice requiring him to furnish such statement within a given time period and he shall furnish the statement within the time specified in the notice;

(IV) Sub-section (4) of said section states that if any person, having furnished a statement, or in pursuance of a notice issued, comes to know or discovers any inaccuracy in the information provided in the statement, he shall within a given period inform the income-tax authority, the inaccuracy in such statement and furnish the correct information in such manner as prescribed;

(V) Sub-section (5) of said section states that the Central Government may, by rules specify the persons to be registered with the prescribed income-tax authority, the nature of information and the manner in which such information shall be maintained by the persons and the due diligence to be carried out by such persons for the purpose of identification of any crypto-asset user or owner;

PROVISIONS RELATING TO TAXATION OF VDA AS PROPOSED IN THE NEW INCOME TAX BILL, 2025

Clause 111 of Section 2 of the Income Tax Bill, 2025 defines Virtual Digital Asset as:

"virtual digital asset" means—

- any information or code or number or token (not being Indian currency or foreign currency), generated through cryptographic means or otherwise, called by any name, providing a digital representation of value exchanged with or without consideration, with the promise or representation of having inherent value, or functions as a store of value or a unit of account including its use in any financial transaction or investment, but not limited to investment scheme; and can be transferred, stored or traded electronically;

- a non-fungible token or any other token of similar nature, by whatever name called;

- any other digital asset, as the Central Government may, by notification, specify,

- any crypto-asset being a digital representation of value that relies on a cryptographically secured distributed ledger or a similar technology to validate and secure transactions, whether or not such asset is included in sub-clause (a) or (b) or (c),

where,--

(i) "non-fungible token" means such digital asset as the Central Government may, by notification, specify;

(ii) the Central Government may, by notification, exclude any digital asset from this definition, subject to such conditions as specified therein;

Income from other sources – Section 92(5)(f) which defines property means the following capital assets of the assessee:-

(i) immovable property being land or building or both;

(ii) shares and securities;

(iii) jewellery;

(iv) archaeological collections;

(v) drawings;

(vi) paintings;

(vii) sculptures;

(viii) any work of art;

(ix) bullion; or

(x) virtual digital asset;

As per this section any immovable property including VDA transferred without consideration, the fair market value of which exceeds fifty thousand rupees, the whole of the aggregate fair market value of such property is taxable as income from other sources.

Transfer of immovable property including VDA transferred for a consideration which is less than the aggregate fair market value of the property by an amount exceeding fifty thousand rupees, the aggregate fair market value of such property as exceeds such consideration is taxable as income from other sources.

Section 104 – Unexplained Asset:

Virtual Digital asset is treated as asset along with money, bullion, jewellery or other valuable article. Where in any tax year, any asset (VDA) has been found to be owned by or belonging to the assessee which is not recorded in the books of account, if any, maintained by such assessee, or the Assessing Officer finds that the amount of such asset exceeds the amount recorded in such books of account where the asset is found recorded, and the assessee––

(a) offers no explanation about the nature and source of acquisition of such asset (VDA), or such excess amount, as the case may be; or

(b) the explanation offered by the assessee, is not satisfactory in the opinion of the Assessing Officer,

then, the value of such asset (VDA), or such excess amount, as the case may be, shall be deemed to be the income of the assessee of the tax year in which such asset has been found to be owned by, or belonging to, the assessee.

Section 194 – Tax on Certain Income:

If any person generates any income from transfer of any VDA is taxable at the rate of 30% subject to following conditions:

(a) No deduction in respect of any expenditure (other than cost of acquisition, if any) or allowance or set off of any loss shall be allowed to the assessee under any provision of this Act in computing the income from VDA.

(b) No set off of loss from transfer of the virtual digital asset computed herein shall be allowed against income computed under any provision of this Act to the assessee and such loss shall not be allowed to be carried forward to succeeding tax years.

Transfer as per Section 2(109):

The term "transfer" as defined in section 2(109), shall apply to any virtual digital asset, whether capital asset or not. As per definition of "Transfer" defined in Section 2(109), if the condition of transfer as set out by Sec 2(109) satisfied then it is treated as transfer irrespective of whether the VDA is recognised as capital asset or as trading asset.

VDA as undisclosed income – Section 301:

Section 301 covers provisions relating to block assessment assessment in case of search or requisition. As per this undisclosed income includes virtual digital asset.

TDS on VDA – Section 393:

If nature of income or any sum by way of consideration for transfer of a virtual digital asset by any person then TDS shall be deducted at the rate of 1%.

TDS is not applicable

Where value or aggregate value of such consideration during the tax year does not exceed--

(a) ₹50,000, when payable by an individual or a Hindu undivided family,—

(i) whose total sales, gross receipts or turnover from the business carried on by him or profession exercised by him does not exceed ₹1,00,00,000 in case of business or ₹50,00,000 in case of profession, during the tax year immediately preceding the tax year in which such virtual digital asset is transferred;

(ii) not having any income under the head "Profits and gains of business or profession";

(b) ₹10,000, when payable by any person other than the person referred to in clause (a).

Possession of VDA – Section 524:

Where any VDA is found to be in possession or control of any person in the course of a search under section 247 or survey under section 253, it may, in any proceeding under this Act, be presumed that such virtual digital asset belong or belongs to such person;

JUDGEMENT OF HON'BLE ITAT JODHPUR BENCH IN THE CASE OF RAUNAQ PRAKASH JAIN

IN THE ITAT JODHPUR BENCH

Raunaq Prakash Jain

v.

Income-tax Officer

DR. S. SEETHALAKSHMI, JUDICIAL MEMBER

AND RATHOD KAMLESH JAYANTBHAI, ACCOUNTANT MEMBER

IT APPEAL NO. 1 (JODH) OF 2024

[ASSESSMENT YEAR 2021-22]

NOVEMBER 28, 2024

Facts of the case:

- The assessee was an individual and salaried person. The assessee purchased Bitcoin (crypto currency) during financial year 2015-16 and sold it during financial year 2020-21. He invested sale consideration inthe purchase of property. The assessee filed return declaring long-term capital gain on sale of Bitcoin andalso claimed exemption under section 54F. The Assessing Officer held that the crypto currency was not a capital asset under section 2(14) and made it taxable under section 56 as the income from other sources.

- On appeal, the Commissioner (Appeals) had held that Crypto Currency (Bitcoins) was not an asset as per section 2(14), hence, the transfer as per section 2(47) as Long-Term Capital Gain was not applicable in the case of the assessee, and accordingly, he also confirmed the deduction denied under section 54F to the assessee.

- The brief facts related to the dispute is that the assessee is a Bachelor of Engineering, had worked with ITcompany Mind Tree Ltd. as well as Infosys Ltd. While in service in 2015-16 he invested a sum of Rs.5.05 lakhs out of his regular income. So the source of investment is not in dispute. The regular source of income of assessee is income from salary, income from other source and income from capital gain on sale of shares/ mutual funds. During the year under consideration assessee offered long-term capital gain on sale of bitcoin at Rs. 6.63 crores and after claiming deduction under section 54F of Rs. 4.95 crores,declaring total income of

Rs. 1.74 crores for tax purpose. The return of income was filed on 30-12-2021.Thereafter, the case of the assessee was selected for complete scrutiny through 'Computer AssistedSelective Scrutiny (CASS)'. The reason for selection in complete scrutiny was 'capital gains deduction claimed' by issuing notice under section 143(2) on 28-6-2022. Notices were issued from time-to-time and were complied by the assessee. The Assessing Officer in the assessment proceeding noted that the assessee has purchased bitcoin (crypto currency) during financial year 2015-16, amounting to Rs. 5.05lakhs and sold bitcoin (crypto currency), during the financial year 2020-21, amounting to Rs. 6.69 crores.Against that sale of bitcoin the assessee claimed indexed cost of purchase of bitcoin for Rs. 5.76 lakhs on purchase of bitcoin, taken set-off of losses from shares Rs. 2,331 and claimed exemption under section 54F amounting to Rs. 4.96 crores. The balance amount of Rs. 1.66 crores was considered as long-term capital gain on the sale of bitcoin and accordingly assessee paid taxes at the rate of 20 per cent. As the reasons for selection of the case was deduction claimed by the assessee the Assessing Officer called from the assessee to explain as to how he is eligible for long-term capital gains, as well as for exemption under section 54F, in accordance with the provisions of the Act from the sale of bitcoin (crypto currency)(virtual digital assets)

Vide notice dated 4-11-2022 issued under section 142(1). The assessee contended that their claim is in accordance with the provision of law and filed a detailed reply. The Assessing Officerconsidered the submission of the assessee, but was not found to be acceptable because the assessee states that he holds bitcoins for more than 3 years and thus claimed the gains on sale as being long-term capital gains. The assessee contended that the bitcoins, (crypto currency) (virtual digital assets) is an asset as per section 2(14), which has been transferred as per provision of section 2(47) and accordingly he has offered the gain arising out of the sale of that asset as long-term capital gains. The Assessing Officer went on observe that as per the amendment made in the Act effective from financial year 2020-21, the bitcoin is nowhere defined as an asset under section 2(14) and accordingly transfer of capital asset under section 2(47) is not applicable in the assessee's case and accordingly the claim of assessee for considering the bitcoins as an asset under section 2(14) and thereby claim of long-term capital gains was not considered.Based on this contention the assessee was asked to show cause as to why the tax on the net gains of Rs.6.63 crores on sale of bitcoins be taxed as 'income from other sources' and accordingly his claim for exemption under section 54F was also not to be considered as allowable. In response the assessee filed a detailed reply not agreeing with the variation proposed in the assessment proceeding and relied on the claim and head of income filed in the return of income, based on the detailed replied filed. The assessee in his reply to the aforesaid show cause notice, contended that as per provision of section 2(14) the assessee owns capital asset and there is not exclusion of the property held by the assessee in that section. Theassessee also contended that as per section 2(14) point (a), it can be concluded that if any property is not explicitly mentioned in the exclusion list of section 2(14), it should be treated as 'capital asset by default considering it as a property of any kind. The Assessing Officer did not find the submission of the assessee acceptable because a bitcoin does not qualifies to be a 'property', such as to be a capital asset within the terms of section 2(14). Since the Act does not define the term 'property', it must be construed in its plainnatural meaning, subject to the context in which that expression occurs and contended that a capital asset is meant to be defined in a wide sense, it yet needs to be a property in the ordinary sense of the word, to

then fall within the definition of a capital asset. In its ordinary sense, a property needs to have inherent benefits, which endows it with value. The Assessing

Officer also noted that to qualify the property or a real asset class, the assessee needs to demonstrate that it is a stocks or an equity interest in a company and a share in its future earnings, bonds to give a promise from a company to pay a certain amount plus interest, an assets having building/structure or a piece of land or that of gold or a precious metal or commodities having utility and value such as oil, gas, metals etc. All the character of the assets was missing in the assets that the assessee contended. The Assessing Officer also contended that these assets are worth on a given day, but they are real things/property that anyway have value, and independent of what the market says, they have inherent value at any moments and that is not so with a cryptocurrency/VDA, where when anyone can buy a crypto or own nothing, except your right to sell your share of nothing to another willing buyer. A crypto, unlike any other property has no independent value or inherent utility and its value is entirely determined by what others will pay or a given day. The AssessingOfficer further went on to observe that a crypto currency is not a currency either. It is not a legal tender. It is merely disruptive and uses technology by either block chain technology, when you buy the crypto token. The bitcoin, therefore, does not own an investment in a real asset class or property, such quality to be an asset, within the meaning of section 2(14). With that reasoning and focusing the amendment made

Vide Finance Act, 2022, wherein revenue releasing the fact that there is no specific provision in the Act to tax the profits/gains of the transactions in virtual digital assets (VDAs), and thus provided to tax suchincome by introducing a new sub-section (47A) in section 2 to define a virtual digital asset and a new section 115BBH to provide for the rate of taxation of gains arising from VDAs, new section 194S for TDSon transactions involving VDAs and the method of computation of such taxable gains simultaneously amending the explanation to section 56(2)(x) and thereby taken a view that the income should be taxed as other income and not as capital gain and consequently the claim of deduction under section 54F was also denied to the assessee.

- When the matter carried before the Commissioner (Appeals) who has held that crypto currency (bitcoins)was not an asset as per section 2(14), hence, the transfer as per section 2(47) as long-term capital gain was not applicable in the case of the appellant and accordingly, he also confirmed the deduction denied under section 54F to the assessee. As regards the contention of the assessee that section 2(14) which defines 'capital asset' as it stood at the time of both the purchase and the sale of crypto currency (bitcoins) does not describe crypto currency (bitcoins) as a capital asset either implicitly or explicitly thereof. The 'virtual digital assets' which contains reference to crypto currencies has only been defined as per section 2(47A)with effect from 1-4-2022 is required to be taxed as incomes falling under residuary status, the same have to be taxed as per section 56. The Commissioner (Appeals) further went on observing that since the section 115BBH inserted by Finance Act, 2022 with effect from 1-4-2023 defines the structure for taxation of such kind of crypto currencies. The intention of the legislature through the section is to allow capital gains in the sale of crypto currencies albeit at a higher rate of 30 per cent without giving the benefit of infrastructure cost while claiming the indexed cost of acquisition and disallowing setting-off losses against any other income and thereby the appeal of the assessee was dismissed.

- Before the Tribunal the assessee effectively taken to ground one that the income be taxed as capital gain and not as other income and if the income be considered as capital gain consequential deduction claimed under section 54F be considered. Plain natural definition of 'property' as is given in the Act property of any kind held by an assessee, whether or not connected with his business or profession; which a person actually owns something of value. Though crypto currency/virtual digital asset is also not a currency but it is not an asset within the meaning of section 2(14). The amendment made in the Finance Act, 2022 has defined virtual digital asset (VDA) under section 2(47A) wherein the name given is of virtual digitalassets. Thus, considering the plan vanilla meaning before the amendment as is to be understood at the time of purchase & sale of crypto currency (bitcoins) which is a right of the assessee attached to the investment made. If the definition of capital asset as given in section 2(14) which say that 'property of any kind held by an assessee, whether or not connected with his business or profession.' Explanation 1 to these sections reads that 'property' includes and shall be deemed to have always included any right in or in relation to an Indian company, including right of management or control or any other right whatsoever.Thus, all rights are property and thereby the right of the assessee in bitcoin though a virtual asset is a capital asset. Therefore, the Assessing Officer is incorrect in holding that to qualify as capital asset one should actually own something as property inasmuch as even if a person has a right or claim on a property it is also a capital asset under section 2(14). Further section 2(47) defines transfer in relation to a capital asset to include sale, exchange or relinquishment or extinguishment of any right therein. Therefore, in the instant case the gain on sale of bitcoin which was acquired by the assessee during financial year 2015-16 for Rs. 5.05 lakhs and sold in financial year 2020-21 for Rs. 6.69 crores results into capital gain and not chargeable under the head income from other sources. It is noted that Finance Act, 2022 with effect from 1-4-2022, the section 2(47A) has been inserted thereby the virtual digital asset meaning was assigned and that including the underlying assets bitcoins. Thus, even the law maker has to clarify that virtual digital asset may be a capital asset and that assets to be treated as income to be taxed as special rate. Even otherwise, if the provision of section 45(1) which says, any profit or gain arising from the transfer of capital assets shall be chargeable to tax as capital gains. Since crypto currency is specifically incorporated in the statute as an asset, it means that even before 1-4-2022 it was an asset and therefore gain on sale of crypto currency has to be taxed under the head capital gain and not under the head income from other sources before the law maker made the specific provision in the Act. Even otherwise, looking to the profile of the assessee it is noted that the only source of income of assessee is from salary and he has invested his savings in shares/crypto currency. He is not regularly dealing in purchase/sale of shares/crypto currency. His intention is to hold for long-term capital gain which is more evident from the fact that he made investment in crypto currency during financial year 2015-16 which was sold in financial year 2020-21 and the gain on sale of crypto currency is invested for purchase of house. This proves that intention of the assessee in making investment in crypto currency is to hold it and to earn long-term capital gain. The revenue has in two cases cited hereinabove has taken a view that the income so earned is taxable under the head capital gain. The same cannot be considered as income from other source merely on the reasons that the assessee by taking that capital gain income also claimed deduction which is otherwise permissible. Thus, even otherwise also when there are two views are possible the view which is favourable to the assessee be considered as held by the Supreme Court in case of CIT Vs. VegetableProducts Ltd. 88 ITR 192. The similar finding is given by the apex court in the case of ChiefCommissioner of CGST Vs. M/s Safari Retreats Pvt. Ltd. Civil Appeal No. 2948 of 2023 order dated 3-10-2024 has held that if two interpretations of a statutory provision are possible, the court ordinarily would interpret the provision in favour of a taxpayer and against the revenue. Therefore also, the gain on sale of crypto currency (bitcoin) prior to assessment year 2022-23 is chargeable to tax as capital gain.

- Next ground raised by the assessee is against the denial of claim of deduction under section 54F on the long-term capital gain declared on sale of crypto currency by taxing such gain under the head income from other sources. As has been held that the income on sale of crypto currency is chargeable to tax under the head long-term capital gain since assessee has hold crypto currency for more than 36 months,therefore, Assessing Officer is directed to allow claim of deduction under section 54F to the assessee.

Order:

Rathod Kamlesh Jayantbhai, Accountant Member.-

By way of the present appeal, the assessee challenges the order of the National Faceless Appeal Centre [NFAC], Delhi dated 04/12/2023 [for short CIT(A)/NFAC]. The appeal relates to the dispute for assessment year 2021-22. That order under challenges arises because the assessee preferred the first appeal against the assessment order dated 26.12.2022 passed under section 143(3)r.w.s. 144B of the Income Tax Act [for short Act] by National Faceless Assessment Unit [for short AO].

2. The present appeal is because, the assessee feels that;

1. "The Ld. CIT(A), NFAC has erred on facts and in law in confirming the action of AO in holding that crypto currency is not a capital asset u/s 2(14) of the IT Act, 1961 in as much as the same is defined byFA, 2022 w.e.f 01.04.2022 u/s 2(47A) of the Act and made taxable u/s 56(2)(x) as income from other sources and thereby taxing gain of Rs. 6,62,96,741/- as income from other sources as against long term capital gain of Rs. 6,62,23,612/-worked out by the assessee and offered for tax.

2. The Ld. CIT(A), NFAC has erred on facts and in law in denying the claim of deduction u/s 54F of Rs.4,95,68,910/- on the long term capital gain declared on sale of crypto currency by

taxing such gain under the head income from other sources.

3.   The assessee craves to amend, alter and modify any of the grounds of appeal."

4.   Succinctly, the fact as culled out from the records is that the assessee is an individual and salaried person.For the year under consideration apart from the salary income, trading / investment in shares and other income, the assessee also offered the income earned on account of sale of Bitcoin (crypto currency). Theassessee filed the return of income on 30.12.2021 declaring total income at Rs. 1,74,39,670/-.

4.1 Subsequent to that the case of the assessee was selected for complete scrutiny through "Computer AssistedSelective Scrutiny (CASS)". The reason for Selection in Complete Scrutiny was "Capital Gains DeductionClaimed" by issuing notice u/s 143(2) of the Act on 28.06.2022. Subsequently, notice u/s 142(1) of the IT Act1961 was issued on various dates along with detailed questionnaire and the same was duly served upon the assessee through e-proceedings on e-filing portal. In response to the various notice issued from time to time the assessee has furnished various details as called for.

4.2 During the course of assessment proceedings, it is seen that the assessee has purchased Bitcoin (CryptoCurrency) during F.Y 2015-16, amounting to Rs. 5,05,155/- and sold Bitcoin (Crypto Currency), during theFY 2020-21, amounting to Rs. 6,69,49,620/-. Against that sale of Bitcoin the assessee claimed indexed cost of purchase of Bitcon for Rs. 5,75,953/- on purchase of Bitcoin, taken set off of losses from shares Rs. 2,331/-and claimed exemption u/s 54F of the Act amounting to Rs. 4,95,68,910/-. The balance amount of Rs.1,66,54,702/- was considered as Long Term Capital Gain on the sale of Bitcoin and accordingly assessee paid taxes @ 20%.

4.3 The ld. AO based on these information asked the assessee to explain as to how he is eligible for long term capital gains, as well as for exemption u/s 54F of the Act, in accordance with the provisions of the Actfrom the sale of Bitcoin (Crypto Currency) (Virtual Digital Assets) vide notice dated 04.11.2022 issued u/s142(1) of the Act which was replied by the assessee on 08.11.22. The ld. AO considered the submission of the assessee, but was not found to be acceptable for the following reasons:

- The assessee states that he holds Bitcoins for more than 3 years and thus claimed the gains on sale as being long term capital gains. The assessee is thus found to have assumed that the

Bitcoins,[Crypto Currency) (Virtual Digital Assets) is an asset as per section 2(14) of the Act, which has been transferred as per section 2(47) of the Act and claimed long term capital gains.

- As per the Act, for FY 2020-21, the Bitcoin is nowhere defined as an asset u/s 2(14) and accordingly transfer of capital asset u/s 2(47) of the Act is not applicable in the assessee's case.

Therefore, the claim of assessee for considering the Bitcoins as an asset u/s 2(14) of the Act and thereby claim of long term capital gains was not considered. Accordingly, a show cause notice dated 15.12.2022 was issued to the assessee, proposing to tax the net gains of Rs. 6,62,96,741/- on sale of Bitcoins as 'Income from other sources' and accordingly his claim for exemption u/s 54F of the Act was not considered as allowable. In response the assessee contended that;

"I would like to clearly and categorically say that I completely disagree with your variation. As in my point of view, I am right in assuming Bitcoin as a 'capital asset and all the other sections including section 54F which are applicable for any capital asset should also be applicable for Bitcoins and gains from sale thereof. I would also like to highlight that as an honest citizen of this country, I have properly and thoroughly declared my gains and income and accordingly filed my taxes and returns promptly, incompleteness, with due diligence and as per the applicable laws.

Lastly I would like to request you for personal hearing for oral submission to present my case through video conferencing."

3.4 The assessee in his reply to the aforesaid show cause notice, contends that section 2(14) point (a) clearly states that capital asset is ANY KIND of property held by an assessee, unless specifically specified in exclusions in section 2(14) points (i) through (vi). As per section 2(14) point (a), it can be concluded that if any property is not explicitly mentioned in the exclusion list of section-2(14), it should be treated as 'capital asset by default considering it as a property of any kind. In accordance with the assessee's request for personal hearing for oral submissions through video conferencing, the same was granted on 21.12.2022, at 12.15 PM, wherein the assessee reiterated his submissions, over Video Conference. His oral submissions during the video conference were similar to those furnished Vide his letter dated 19.12.2022. Finally the ld. AO noted written and oral submissions have been carefully considered, but were not found to be acceptable for reasons discussed hereunder:

- The assessee's primary contention is that section 2(14) point (a) clearly states that a 'capital asset' is any kind of property held by an assessee unless specifically specified in exclusions in section 2(14),point (i) through (vi).

- The question therefore is whether a Bitcoin qualifies to be a 'property', such as to be a capital asset within the terms of section 2(14) of the Act. Since the Act does not define the term 'property', it must be construed in its plain natural meaning, subject to the context in which that expression occurs (ref. to JK Trust v. CIT/EPT, 23 ITR 150, Bom). While a capital asset is meant to be defined in a wide sense, it yet needs to be a property in the ordinary sense of the word, to then fall within the definition of a capital asset. In its ordinary sense, a property needs to have inherent benefits,which endows it with value.

- It is trite knowledge, that with property or a real asset class, you actually own something of value eg.

  - Stocks-give an equity Interest in a company and a share in its future earnings.

  - bonds-give a promise from a company to pay a certain amount plus interest.

- real estate–gives a building/structure or a piece of land.

- gold-is a precious metal.

- commodities – have utility and value (such as oil, gas, metals etc.)

While the market determines what these assets are worth on a given day, but they are realthings/property that anyway have value, and independent of what the market says, they have inherent value at any moments That is not so with a crypto currency/VDA, where when you buy a crypto you own nothing, except your right to sell your share of nothing to another willing buyer. Acrypto, unlike any other property has no independent value or inherent utility and its value is entirely determined by what others will pay or a given day.

- A crypto currency is not a currency either. It is not a legal tender. It is merely disruptive and uses technology by either block chain technology, when you buy the crypto token. The Bitcoin, therefore, does not own an investment in a real asset class or property, such as to quality to be an asset, within the meaning of section 2(14) of the Act.

- It is for this reason, that the Finance Act 2022, recognised that there is no specific provision in theAct to tax the profits/gains of the transactions in Virtual Digital Assets (VDAs), and thus provided to tax such income by introducing (i) a new sub section (47A) in section 2 to define a virtual digital asset, (ii) a new section 115BBH to provide for the rate of taxation of gains arising from VDAs and the method of computation of such taxable gains (iii) amended the explanation to section 56(2)(x),new section 1948 for TDS on transactions Involving VDAs. to include VDAs and (iv) Introduced anew section 194S for TDS on transactions involving VDAs.

4.5 Based on reasons discussed herein above, the assessee's primary contention that Bitcoin is a capital asset within the meaning of section 2(14) of the Act and that the gains arising there under be taxed as capital gains was rejected and the said gains was taxed as Income from other sources as under-

Total sale Consideration (from Bitcoin)		Amount (in Rs.) 6,69,49,620/-
Less: (i) Cost of acquisition	5,05,155/-	
(ii) Related Expenses	1,47,724/-	6,52,879/-

Net gains taxed under the head 'Income from other sources'		6,62,96,741/-

Accordingly, the assessee's claim for exemption u/s 54F of the Act was also rejected.

5. Aggrieved from the above finding of the Assessing Officer, the assessee preferred an appeal before the ld.CIT(A). Ld. CIT(A) after considering the arguments and submission filed by the assessee disposed the appeal of the assessee by holding as under:-

"5. Decision:-

Ground No.1:- The only ground of appeal is an addition of Rs. Rs.6,62,96,741/- by the Ld. AO by not treating the sale of Crypto Currency of Rs.6,69,49,620/- as long term capital asset and taxed as 'IncomeFrom Other Sources.'

As per the facts of the case, during the course of assessment proceedings, the Ld. AO observed that assessee had purchased Crypto Currency (Bitcoins) during F.Y.2015-16 amounting to Rs.5,05,155/- andsold the same during the F.Y.2020-21 at a consideration of Rs.6,69,49,620/- after claiming indexed cost of Rs.5,75,953/- on the purchase of Bitcoin, having also taken the set off of losses from shares ofRs.2,331/-. The appellant further claimed an exemption u/s 54F of the Act amounting toRs.4,95,68,910/-, thereby offering Rs. 1,66,54,702/- as Long Term Capital Gains on the sale of Bitcoins at the tax rate of 20%. The Ld. AO contended that Crypto Currency (Bitcoins) was not an asset as per section 2(14) of the Act, hence, the transfer as per section 2(47) as Long Term Capital Gain was not applicable in the case of the appellant. The Id. AO accordingly disallowed the claim of exemption u/s54F of the assessee and made the impugned addition thereof under the head 'Income From OtherSources'.

The facts of the case and the submission of the appellant have been considered. Section 2(14) of the Act which defines "Capital Asset" as it stood at the time of both the purchase and the sale of Crypto Currency (Bitcoins) does not describe Crypto Currency (Bitcoins) as a Capital Asset either implicitly or explicitly thereof. The "Virtual Digital Assets" which contains reference to Crypto Currencies has only been defined as per section 2(47A) of the Act with effect from 01.04.2022.

In such cases of incomes falling under residuary status, the same have to be taxed as per section 56 of theAct. Hence, the action of Ld. AO in denying the benefit of section 54F as per Long Term Capital Gains is seems to be logical.

The appellant has annexed the assessment orders in the cases of Ashok Kumar Asawa and Prakash Chand Jain (Father of the appellant) wherein the income has been taxed as Long Term Capital Gain by the Ld.AO treating Crypto Currency as Capital Asset u/s 2(14) of the Act. Since, these are assessment orders which were adjudicated by different Ld. AO and not a matter of appeal before me, I have no comments to offer on the same. Further, there can be different views on interpretation of provisions of Act, this is how the law develops, the views on a legal subject can not be restrict to a water tight compartment. The can be dynamic and incongruent.

Further, section 115BBH inserted by Finance Act 2022 w.e.f. 01.04.2023 defines the structure for taxation of such kind of Crypto Currencies. The intention of the legislature through the section is to allowCapital Gains in the sale of Crypto Currencies albeit at a higher rate of 30% without giving the benefit of infrastructure cost while claiming the indexed cost of acquisition and disallowing setting off losses against any other income.

In view of the discussion the addition made by the Ld. AO of Rs.6,62,96,741/-is hereby confirmed. The Ground of appeal no. 1 is hereby dismissed."

6. As the assessee did not find any favour, from the appeal so filed before the ld. CIT(A)/NFAC, the assessee

has preferred the present appeal before this Tribunal on the ground as reproduced hereinabove. The ld. AR of the assessee in support of the various grounds so raised has filed the written submission which reads as follows:

1. The assessee did his Bachelor of Engineering from Bangalore in computer & information science in the year 2004. He worked with IT company Mind Tree Ltd. as software developer from 2004 to 2009.Thereafter he did his MBA in 2012 and joined Infosys Ltd. as senior software consultant and IT project manager till 2024. Presently he has lost his job at Infosys and unemployed.

2. The regular source of income of assessee is income from salary and from capital gain on sale of shares/ mutual funds. During the year under consideration assessee earned long term capital gain on sale of bitcoin at Rs.6,63,73,667/- and after claiming deduction u/s 54F of Rs.4,95,68,910/-, filed the return on 30.12.2021 declaring total income of Rs.1,74,39,670/-.

3. The AO at Para 3.8 of the order observed that Act has not defined the term 'property' and therefore it must be construed in its plain natural meaning. With a property, a person actually owns something of value. This is

not so with crypto currency/ virtual digital asset. Crypto currency is also not a currency. Therefore, it is not an asset within the meaning of section 2(14) of the Act. FA, 2022 has defined VirtualDigital Asset (VDA) u/s 2(47A) of the Act and the rate of taxation on gain from VDA is provided by section 115BBH of the Act. Accordingly AO computed gain on sale of bitcoin at Rs.6,62,96,741/- and taxed the same under the head income from other sources.

4. The Ld. CIT(A), NFAC observed that section 2(14) as it stood at the time of purchase & sale of cryptocurrency (bitcoins) does not described it as a capital asset either implicitly or explicitly. The VDA is defined u/s 2(47A) only w.e.f. 01.04.2022 and therefore, the income falling under residuary status has to be taxed u/s 56 of the Act. Further the assessment order in case of Ashok Kumar Asawa and Prakash Chandra Jain where gain from crypto currency was taxed under the head capital gain, since these assessment orders were passed by a different AO and not a matter of appeal, he refrained from offering any comment. Accordingly the order passed by AO is upheld.

Submission:

1. The only issue in the present case is whether crypto currency (bitcoin) is a capital asset or not. The capital asset is defined u/s 2(14) of the Act to mean "Property of any kind held by an assessee, whether or not connected with his business or profession." Explanation 1 to this sections reads as under:-

    For the removal of doubts, it is hereby clarified that "property" includes and shall be deemed to have always included any right in or in relation to an Indian company, including right of management or control or any other right whatsoever.

    Thus all rights are property and thereby is a capital asset. Therefore, the AO is incorrect in holding that to qualify as capital asset one should actually own something as property in as much as even if a person hasa right or claim on a property it is also a capital asset u/s 2(14) of the Act. Further section 2(47) of the Act defines transfer in relation to a capital asset to include sale, exchange or relinquishment or extinguishment of any right therein. Therefore in the present case the gain on sale of bitcoin which was acquired by the assessee during FY

2015-16 for Rs.5,05,155/- and sold in FY 2020-21 forRs.6,69,49,620/- results into capital gain and not chargeable under the head income from other sources.

2. It may be noted that by FA, 2022 w.e.f. 01.04.2022, following sections were introduced in the FA to deal with the taxation of Virtual Digital Asset.

Section 2(47A)- Virtual Digital Asset means:-

- any information or code or number or token (not being Indian currency or foreign currency),generated through cryptographic means or otherwise, by whatever name called, providing a digital representation of value exchanged with or without consideration, with the promise or representation of having inherent value, or functions as a store of value or a unit of account including its use in any financial transaction or investment, but not limited to investment scheme; and can be transferred, stored or traded electronically;

- a non-fungible token or any other token of similar nature, by whatever name called;

- any other digital asset, as the Central Government may, by notification in the Official Gazette Specify:

Provided that the Central Government may, by notification in the Official Gazette, exclude any digitalasset from the definition of virtual digital asset subject to such conditions as may be specified therein.

Explanation--For the purposes of this clause -

- "non-fungible token" means such digital asset as the Central Government may, by notification in theOfficial Gazette, specify;

- the expressions "currency", "foreign currency" and "Indian currency" shall have the same meanings as respectively assigned to them in clauses (h), (m) and (q) of section 2 of the Foreign ExchangeManagement Act, 1999.]

Thus as per section 2(47A) also, crypto currency is specifically considered as an asset. Further section 115BBH(3) which deals with taxation of income from VDA provides that "For the purposes of this section, the ward "transfer" as defined in clause (47) of section 2, shall apply to any virtual digital asset(VDA), whether capital assets or not".

Thus it is clear that even the legislature has clarified that virtual digital asset may be a capital asset.

3. As per section 45(1), any profit or gain arising from the transfer of capital assets shall be chargeable to tax as Capital Gains. Since crypto currency is specifically incorporated in the statute as an asset, it means that even before 01.04.2022 it was an asset and therefore gain on sale of crypto currency has to be taxed under the head capital gain and not under the head income from other sources.

4. The Ld. CIT(A) has referred to section 56 of Income tax Act which provides that "Income of every kind which is not to be excluded from the total income under this Act shall be chargeable to income-tax under the head "Income from other sources", if it is not chargeable to income-tax under any of the head specified in section 14, items A to E (i.e. Salaries, Income From house property, Profit and gains of business or profession, Capital Gain). In the present case, gain on sale of crypto currency is chargeable to tax under the head Capital Gain and therefore it cannot be charged to tax under the head income from other sources.

5. We may further submit that the only source of income of assessee is from salary and he has invested his savings in shares/ crypto currency. He is not regularly dealing in purchase/ sale of shares/ cryptocurrency. His intention is to hold for long term capital gain which is more evident from the fact that he made investment in

crypto currency during FY 2015-16 which was sold in FY 2020-21 and the gain on sale of crypto currency is invested for purchase of house. This proves that intention of the assessee in making investment in crypto currency is to hold it and to earn long term capital gain.

6. It is further submitted that even the AO in case of Sh. Ashok Kumar Asawa for AY 2018-19 and in case of Sh. Prakash Chand Jain for AY 2018-19 has taxed the gain on sale of crypto currency under the head capital gain. The relevant extracts of these assessment orders is as under:-

In case of Sh. Ashok Kumar Asawa:

Para 4.6- Conclusion Drawn:

Keeping in view of the said facts of the case, it is concluded that assessee has earned STCG in trading ofCrypto Currency at Rs. 2,42,892/-, over and above the STCG shown in his ITR and the same has been further admitted vide his reply submitted on 16.03.2023, is being added to his taxable income for the assessment year 2018-19 and charged tax accordingly."

In case of Prakash Chand Jain:

"In view of the above, the Virtual/Digital/Crypto Currency transactions cannot be termed as currency transactions or securities trading or commodity trading and the same would be treated as Capital Asset.Section

2(14) of I.T. Act 1961 defines capital asset as property of any kind held by an assessee, whether or not connected with his business or profession. "

7. Otherwise also, Hon'ble Supreme Court in case of CIT v. Vegetable Products Ltd. [1973] 88 ITR 192(SC) has held that where two reasonable constructions of a taxing provision are possible, then the construction which favours the assessee must be adopted. Further Hon'ble Supreme Court in case of Chief Commissioner of CGST v. M/s Safari Retreats Pvt. Ltd. Civil Appeal No. 2948 of 2023 order dt.03.10.2024 at page 32, para 25(d) has held that if two interpretations of a statutory provision are possible,the court ordinarily would interpret the provision in favour of a taxpayer and against the revenue.Therefore also, the gain on sale of crypto currency (bitcoin) prior to AY 2022-23 is chargeable to tax as capital gain.

Ground No.2:

The Ld. CIT(A), NFAC has erred on facts and in law in denying the claim of deduction u/s 54F of Rs.4,95,68,910/- on the long term capital gain declared on sale of crypto currency by taxing such gain under the head income from other sources.

Facts & Submission:

1. Since AO treated the gain on sale of crypto currency as chargeable to tax under the head income from other sources, he did not allowed deduction u/s 54F of the Act.

2. As submitted above, the gain on sale of crypto currency is chargeable to tax under the head long term capital gain since assessee has hold crypto currency for more than 36 months, therefore, AO be directed to allow claim of deduction u/s 54F of the Act."

3. The ld. AR of the assessee in addition to the above written submission so filed vehemently argued that the assessee is salaried employee. Assessee after completing the B. E. in Computer science worked in Mind tree2004-2009 and thereafter when he completed his MBA he joined Infosys. While in service in 2015-16 he invested a sum of Rs. 5,05,155/- out of his regular income. So the source of investment is not in dispute. In the assessment proceeding the assessee filed a detailed submission stating that as to how this transaction is chargeable to tax under the head Capital Gain. The ld. AR of the assessee stated that in the amendment made in the law has given the transaction name as Virtual Digital

Assets[VDA]. So till the law amendment even the law makers consider that as the VDA. So merely the law has been amended subsequently that law does not apply retrospectively and the intention of the assessee was to invest his tax paid as an investment and the gain which he has offered cannot be considered as other income and thereby denial of benefit of capital assets is not in accordance with law. To drive home to this contention ld. AR of the assessee invited out attention to the definition clause 2(47) & 2(47A) and provision of section 14, 56 and provision of section 115BBH and submitted that even the law recognise it as assets but subsequently intended to charge as other income which are prospective in nature. Therefore, the treatment given by the assessee be accepted as capital assets in the hands of the assessee. The ld. AR of the assessee also invited attention to the assessment order of AhokkumarAsawa (AFHPA7809P) wherein similar issue was decided by the national faceless assessment unit as capital assets Vide para 4.6 of that order placed on record and submitted that when two views are possible view favourable to the assessee be taken as held by the apex court in the case of Vegetable Products Ltd. The ld.AR also relied on the finding of apex court in the case of Safari Retreats P. Ltd.(supra). If the contention of the assessee for capital assets is accepted then issue of deduction u/s.54F is consequential in nature.

4. The ld DR is heard who relied on the findings of the lower authorities and more particularly advanced the similar contentions as stated in the order of the ld. CIT(A). The ld. DR vehemently submitted that the assessee dealt with the dark web illegal transaction which was not recognised transaction and there cannot be capital gain in the hands of the assessee. Even the RBI has cautioned the public not to deal with such type of transactions. The transaction undertaken by the assessee does not fall in the legal definition given under theAct for capital assets. Even the law has recognised such type of transaction as other income and to be taxed as other income.

5. We have heard the rival contentions and perused the material placed on record. In this appeal the assessee has effectively taken two grounds which are interrelated and deal with the chargeability of gain on sale of bitcoin which was acquired by the assessee during financial year 2015-16 for Rs.5,05,155/- and sold in FY

2020-21 for Rs.6,69,49,620/-. The mute question that is to be decided as to whether the proceeds received on sale of Bitcoin is chargeable to tax as capital gain or income from other source. The brief facts related to the dispute is that the assessee is a Bachelor of Engineering, had worked with IT company Mind Tree Ltd. as well as Infosys Ltd. While in service in 2015-16 he invested a sum of Rs. 5,05,155/- out of his regular income. Sothe source of investment is not in dispute. The regular source of income of assessee is income from salary,Income from other source and income from capital gain on sale of shares/ mutual funds. During the year under consideration assessee offered long term capital gain on sale of bitcoin at Rs.6,63,73,667/- and after claiming deduction u/s 54F of Rs.4,95,68,910/-, declaring total income of Rs.1,74,39,670/- for tax purpose.The return of income was filed on 30.12.2021.

Thereafter, the case of the assessee was selected for complete scrutiny through "Computer Assisted SelectiveScrutiny (CASS)". The reason for Selection in Complete Scrutiny was "Capital Gains Deduction Claimed" by issuing notice u/s 143(2) of the Act on 28.06.2022. Notices were issued from time to time and were compiled by the assessee. The ld. AO in the assessment proceeding noted that the the assessee has purchased Bitcoin(Crypto Currency) during F.Y 2015-16, amounting to Rs. 5,05,155/- and sold Bitcoin (Crypto Currency),during the FY 202021, amounting to Rs. 6,69,49,620/-. Against that sale of Bitcoin the assessee claimed indexed cost of purchase of Bitcon for Rs. 5,75,953/-on purchase of Bitcoin, taken set off of losses from shares Rs. 2,331/-and claimed exemption u/s 54F of the Act amounting to Rs. 4,95,68,910/-. The balance amount of Rs. 1,66,54,702/- was considered as Long Term Capital Gain on the sale of Bitcoin and accordingly assessee paid taxes @ 20%. As the reasons for selection of the case was deduction claimed by the assessee the ld. AO called from the assessee to explain as to how he is eligible for long term capital gains, as well as for exemption u/s 54F of the Act, in accordance with the provisions of the Act from the sale of Bitcoin(Crypto Currency) (Virtual Digital Assets) vide notice dated 04.11.2022 issued u/s 142(1) of the Act. Theassessee contended that their claim is in accordance with the provision of law and filed a detailed reply. The ld. AO considered the submission of the assessee, but was not found to be acceptable because the assessee states that he holds Bitcoins for more than 3 years and thus claimed the gains on sale as being long term capital gains. The assessee contended that the Bitcoins, [Crypto Currency) (Virtual Digital Assets) is an asset as per section 2(14) of the Act, which has been transferred as per provision of section 2(47) of the Act and accordingly he has offered the gain arising out of the sale of that asset as long term capital gains. The ld. AO went on to observe that as per the amendment made in the Act effective from financial year 2020-21, theBitcoin is nowhere defined as an asset u/s 2(14) and accordingly transfer of capital asset u/s 2(47) of the Actis not applicable in the assessee's case and accordingly the claim of assessee for considering the Bitcoins as an asset u/s 2(14) of the Act and thereby claim of long term capital gains was not considered. Based on these contention the assessee was asked to show cause on 15.12.2022 as to why the tax on the net gains of Rs.6,62,96,741/- on sale of Bitcoins be taxed as 'Income from other sources' and accordingly his claim for exemption u/s 54F of the Act was also not to be considered as allowable. In response the assessee filed a detailed reply not agreeing with the variation proposed in the assessment proceeding and relied on the claim and head of income filed in the return of income, based on the detailed replied filed. The assessee in his reply to the aforesaid show cause notice, contended that as per provision of section 2(14) the assessee owns capital asset and there is not exclusion of the property held by the assessee in that section. The assessee also contended that as per section 2(14) point (a), it can be concluded that if any property is not explicitly mentioned in the exclusion list of section 2(14), it should be treated as 'capital asset by default considering it as a property of any kind.

The ld. AO did not find the submission of the assessee acceptable because a Bitcoin does not qualifies to be a property', such as to be a capital asset within the terms of section 2(14) of the Act. Since the Act does not define the term 'property', it must be construed in its plain natural meaning, subject to the context in whichthat expression occurs (Ref. to JK Trust v. CIT/ EPT, 23 ITR 150, Bom) and contended that a capital asset is meant to be defined in a wide sense, it yet needs to be a property in the ordinary sense of the word, to then fall within the definition of a capital asset. In its ordinary sense, a property needs to have inherent benefits, whichendows it with value. The ld. AO also noted that to qualify the property or a real asset class, the assessee needs to demonstrate that it is a Stocks or an equity Interest in a company and a share in its future earnings,bonds to give a promise from a company to pay a certain amount plus interest, an assets having building /structure or a piece of land or that of gold or a precious metal or commodities having utility and value such as oil, gas, metals etc. All the character of the assets was missing in the assets that the assessee contended. The ld. AO also contended that these assets are worth on a given day, but they are real things/property that anyway have value, and independent of what the market says, they have inherent value at any moments and that is not so with a crypto currency/VDA, where when anyone can buy a crypto or own nothing, except your right to sell your share of nothing to another willing buyer. A crypto, unlike any other property has no independent value or inherent utility and its value is entirely determined by what others will pay or a given day. The ld. AO further went on to observe that a crypto currency is not a currency either. It is not a legal tender. It is merely disruptive and uses technology by either block chain technology, when you buy the crypto token. The Bitcoin,therefore, does not own an investment in a real asset class or property, such as to quality to be an asset, within the meaning of section 2(14) of the Act. With that reasoning and focusing the amendment made

Vide:

FinanceAct 2022, wherein revenue releasing the fact that there is no specific provision in the Act to tax the profits/gains of the transactions in Virtual Digital Assets (VDAs), and thus provided to tax such income by introducing (i) a new sub section (47A) in section 2 to define a virtual digital asset and a new section 115BB to provide for the rate of taxation of gains arising from VDAs, new section 194S for TDS on transactionsInvolving VDAs and the method of computation of such taxable gains simultaneously amending the the explanation to section 56(2)(x) and thereby taken a view that the income should be taxed as other income and not as capital gain and consequently the claim of deduction u/s.54F was also denied to the assessee.

When the matter carried before the ld. CIT(A) who has held that Crypto Currency (Bitcoins) was not an asset as per section 2(14) of the Act, hence, the transfer as per section 2(47) as Long Term Capital Gain was not applicable in the case of the appellant and accordingly he also confirmed the deduction denied u/s. 54F to theassessee. As regards the contention of the assessee that Section 2(14) of the Act which defines "Capital Asset"as it stood at the time of both the purchase and the sale of Crypto Currency (Bitcoins) does not describeCrypto Currency (Bitcoins) as a Capital Asset either implicitly or explicitly thereof. The "Virtual DigitalAssets" which contains reference to Crypto Currencies has only been defined as per section 2(47A) of the Actwith effect from 01.04.2022 is required to be taxed as incomes falling under residuary status, the same have to be taxed as per section 56 of the Act. As regards the reliance of similar issue decided in the case of otherassessee Shri Ashok Kumar Asawa and

Prakash Chand Jain (Father of the appellant) wherein the income has been taxed as Long Term

Capital Gain by the Ld. AO treating Crypto Currency as Capital Asset u/s 2(14) of the Act. Since, these are assessment orders which were adjudicated by different Ld. AO and not a matter of appeal before him, he has not considered the plea of the assessee. The ld. CIT(A) further went on observing that since the section section 115BBH inserted by Finance Act 2022 w.e.f. 01.04.2023 defines the structure for taxation of such kind of Crypto Currencies. The intention of the legislature through the section is to allowCapital Gains in the sale of Crypto Currencies albeit at a higher rate of 30% without giving the benefit of infrastructure cost while claiming the indexed cost of acquisition and disallowing setting off losses against any other income and thereby the appeal of the assessee was dismissed.

Before us as we note that the assessee effectively taken to ground one that the income be taxed as capital gain and not as other income and if the income be considered as capital gain consequential deduction claimed u/s.54F be considered. Before we proceed to decide the first issue we would like refer to the connected provisions of law as applicable to the year under dispute. First we refer the provision of section 2(14) and 2 (47) of theAct which reads as under:

Section 2(14):

(14) "capital asset" means—

a.   property of any kind held by an assessee, whether or not connected with his business or profession;

b.   any securities held by a Foreign Institutional Investor which has invested in such securities in accordance with the regulations made under the Securities and Exchange Board of India Act, 1992(15 of 1992);

c.   any unit linked insurance policy to which exemption under clause (10D) of section 10 does not apply on account of the applicability of the fourth and fifth provisos thereof, but does not include—

- any stock-in-trade [other than the securities referred to in sub-clause (b)], consumable stores or raw materials held for the purposes of his business or profession;

- personal effects, that is to say, movable property (including wearing apparel and furniture) held for personal use by the assessee or any member of his family dependent on him, but excludes—

(a) jewellery;

(b) archaeological collections;

(c) drawings;

(d) paintings;

(e) sculptures; or

(f) any work of art.

Explanation.—For the purposes of this sub-clause, "jewellery" includes—

- ornaments made of gold, silver, platinum or any other precious metal or any alloy containing one or more of such precious metals, whether or not containing any precious or semi-precious stone, and whether or not worked or sewn into any wearing apparel;

- precious or semi-precious stones, whether or not set in any furniture, utensil or other article or worked or sewn into any wearing apparel;

(iii) agricultural land in India, not being land situate—

xxx xxx xxx xxx

(iv) 6 1/2 per cent Gold Bonds, 1977, or 7 per cent Gold Bonds, 1980, or National Defence Gold Bonds,1980, issued by the Central Government;

(v) Special Bearer Bonds, 1991, issued by the Central Government;

(vi) Gold Deposit Bonds issued under the Gold Deposit Scheme, 1999 or deposit certificates issued under the Gold Monetisation Scheme, 2015 notified by the Central Government.

Explanation 1.—For the removal of doubts, it is hereby clarified that "property" includes and shall be deemed to have always included any rights in or in relation to an Indian company, including rights of management or control or any other rights whatsoever.

Explanation 2.—For the purposes of this clause—

- the expression "Foreign Institutional Investor" shall have the meaning assigned to it in clause (a) of the Explanation to section 115AD;

- the expression "securities" shall have the meaning assigned to it in clause (h) of section 2 of theSecurities Contracts (Regulation) Act, 1956 (42 of 1956);

Section 2(47)

(47) "transfer", in relation to a capital asset, includes,—

i. the sale, exchange or relinquishment of the asset; or

ii. the extinguishment of any rights therein; or

iii. the compulsory acquisition thereof under any law; or

iv. in a case where the asset is converted by the owner thereof into, or is treated by him as, stock-in-trade of a business carried on by him, such conversion or treatment; or

iva. the maturity or redemption of a zero coupon bond; or

v. any transaction involving the allowing of the possession of any immovable property to be taken or retained in part performance of a contract of the nature referred to in section 53A of the Transfer ofProperty Act, 1882 (4 of 1882); or

vi. any transaction (whether by way of becoming a member of, or acquiring shares in, a co-operative society, company or other association of persons or by way of any agreement or any arrangement orin any other manner whatsoever) which has the effect of transferring, or enabling the enjoyment of,any immovable property.

Explanation 1.—For the purposes of sub-clauses (v) and (vi), "immovable property" shall have the same meaning as in clause (d) of section 269UA.

Explanation 2.—For the removal of doubts, it is hereby clarified that "transfer" includes and shall be deemed to have always included disposing of or parting with an asset or any interest therein, or creating any interest in any asset in any manner whatsoever, directly or indirectly, absolutely or conditionally, voluntarily or involuntarily, by way of an agreement (whether entered into in India or outside India) or otherwise, notwithstanding that such transfer of rights has been characterised as being effected or dependent upon or flowing from the transfer of a share or shares of a company registered or incorporated outside India;

Plain natural definition of 'property' as is given in the Act property of any kind held by an assessee, whether or not connected with his business or profession; which a person actually owns something of value. Though currency / virtual digital asset is also not a currency but it is not an asset within the meaning of section 2(14) of the Act. The amendment made in the Finance Act, 2022 has defined Virtual Digital Asset (VDA) u/s 2(47A) of the Act wherein the name given is of virtual digital assets. Thus, considering the plan vanilla meaning before the amendment as is to be understood at the time of purchase & sale of crypto currency(bitcoins) which is a right of the assessee attached to the investment made. If we consider the definition of capital asset as given in section 2(14) of the Act which say that "Property of any kind held by an assessee,whether or not connected with his business or profession." Explanation 1 to this sections reads that "property"includes and shall be deemed to have always included any right in or in relation to an Indian company,including right of management or control or any other right whatsoever. Thus all rights are property and thereby the right of the assessee in Bitcon though a virtual assets is a capital asset.

Therefore, the AO is incorrect in holding that to qualify as capital asset one should actually own something as property in as much as even if a person has a right or claim on a property it is also a capital asset u/s 2(14) of the Act. Further section 2(47) of the Act defines transfer in relation to a capital asset to include sale, exchange or relinquishment or extinguishment of any right therein. Therefore in the present case the gain on sale of bitcoin which was acquired by the assessee during FY 2015-16 for Rs.5,05,155/- and sold in FY 2020-21 forRs.6,69,49,620/-results into capital gain and not chargeable under the head income from other sources. We Note that Finance Act, 2022 w.e.f. 01.04.2022, the section 2(47A) has been inserted thereby the Virtual DigitalAsset meaning was assigned and that including the underlying assets Bitcoins. Thus even the law maker has to clarify that virtual digital asset may be a capital asset and that assets to be treated as income to be taxed as special rate. The relevant amendment in the law is prospective as is evident from the memorandum explaining the budgetary provision which reads as under:

Scheme for taxation of virtual digital assets:

Virtual digital assets have gained tremendous popularity in recent times and the volumes of trading in such digital assets has increased substantially. Further, a market is emerging where payment for the transfer of a virtual digital asset can be made through another such asset. Accordingly, a new scheme to provide for taxation of such virtual digital assets has been proposed in the Bill.

2. The proposed section 115BBH seeks to provide that where the total income of an assessee includes any income from transfer of any virtual digital asset, the income tax payable shall be the aggregate of the amount of income-tax calculated on income of transfer of any virtual digital asset at the rate of 30% and the amount of income-tax with which the assessee would have been chargeable had the total income of the assessee been reduced by the aggregate of the income from transfer of virtual digital asset.

2.1 However, no deduction in respect of any expenditure (other than cost of acquisition) or allowance or set off of any loss shall be allowed to the assessee under any provision of the Act while computing income from transfer of such asset.

2.2 Further, no set off of any loss arising from transfer of virtual digital asset shall be allowed against any income computed under any other provision of the Act and such loss shall not be allowed to be carried forward to subsequent assessment years.

2.3 This amendment will take effect from 1 st April, 2023 and will accordingly apply in relation to the assessment year 2023-24 and subsequent assessment years.

Even otherwise, if we further peruse provision of section 45(1) which says, any profit or gain arising from the transfer of capital assets shall be chargeable to tax as Capital Gains. Since crypto currency is specifically incorporated in the statute as an asset, it means that even before 01.04.2022 it was an asset and therefore gain on sale of crypto currency has to be taxed under the head capital gain and not under the head income from other sources before the law maker made the specific provision in the Act. Even otherwise, looking to the profile of the assessee we note that the only source of income of assessee is from salary and he has invested his savings in shares / crypto currency. He is not regularly dealing in purchase/ sale of shares/ crypto currency.His intention is to hold for long term capital gain which is more evident from the fact that he made investment in crypto currency during FY 2015-16 which was sold in FY 2020-21 and the gain on sale of crypto currency is invested for purchase of house. This proves that intention of the assessee in making investment in cryptocurrency is to hold it and to earn long term capital gain.

Before us the ld. AR of the assessee filed the copy of the assessment order of Shri Ashok Kumar Asawa forAY 2018-19 and in case of Sh. Prakash Chand Jain for AY 2018-19 wherein the similar income was taxed as capital gain. The relevant extracts of these assessment orders reads as under:-

In case of Sh. Ashok Kumar Asawa

Para 4.6- Conclusion Drawn.

Keeping in view of the said facts of the case, it is concluded that assessee has earned STCG in trading ofCrypto Currency at Rs. 2,42,892/-, over and above the STCG shown in his ITR and the same has been further admitted vide his reply submitted on 16.03.2023, is being added to his taxable income for the assessment year 2018-19 and charged tax accordingly."

In case of Prakash Chand Jain

"In view of the above, the Virtual/Digital/Crypto Currency transactions cannot be termed as currency transactions or securities trading or commodity trading and the same would be treated as Capital Asset.

Section 2(14) of I.T. Act 1961 defines capital asset as property of any kind held by an assessee, whether or not connected with his business or profession. "

As we note that the revenue has in two cases cited herein above has taken a view that the income so earned is taxable under the head capital gain. The same cannot be considered as income from other source merely on the reasons that the assessee by taking that capital gain income also claimed deduction which is otherwise permissible.

Thus, even otherwise also when there are two views are possible the view which is favorable to the assessee be considered as held by the Hon'ble Supreme Court in case of CIT v. Vegetable Products Ltd. [1973] 88 ITR192 (SC). The similar finding is given by the apex court in the case of Chief Commissioner of CGST v. M/sSafari Retreats Pvt. Ltd. Civil Appeal No. 2948 of 2023 order dt. 03.10.2024 at page 32, para 25(d) has held that if two interpretations of a statutory provision are possible, the court ordinarily would interpret the provision in favour of a taxpayer and against the revenue. Therefore also, the gain on sale of crypto currency(bitcoin) prior to AY 2022-23 is chargeable to tax as capital gain. Based on the discussion so recorded ground no. 1 raised by the assessee is allowed.

Ground no. 2 raised by the assessee raised by the assessee is against the denial of claim of deduction u/s 54Fof Rs.4,95,68,910/- on the long term capital gain declared on sale of crypto currency by taxing such gain under the head income from other sources. As we have in ground no. 1 held that the income on sale of cryptocurrency is chargeable to tax under the head long term capital gain since assessee has hold crypto currency for more than 36 months, therefore, AO is directed to allow claim of deduction u/s 54F of the Act to the assessee.

Based on this observation ground no. 2 raised by the assessee is allowed.

Ground no. 3 being general in nature does not require any finding.

In the result, the appeal of the assessee is allowed.